Bringing Lent Home with
St. John Paul II

Prayers, Reflections, and

Activities for Families

Donna-Marie Cooper O'Boyle

ave maria press AMP **notre dame, indiana**

Also in the
BRINGING LENT HOME
S E R I E S

Bringing Lent Home
with St. Thérèse of Lisieux
ISBN: 978-1-59471-421-4

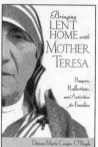

Bringing Lent Home
with Mother Teresa
ISBN: 978-1-59471-286-9

available at **www.avemariapress.com**

Founded in 1865, Ave Maria Press is a ministry of the United States Province of Holy Cross.

www.avemariapress.com

Paperback: ISBN-13 978-1-59471-560-0

E-book: ISBN-13 978-1-59471-561-7

Cover image © Martin Athenstaedt/dpa/Corbis.

Cover and text design by Katherine Coleman.

Printed and bound in the United States of America.

Lovingly, for my children:

Justin,

Chaldea,

Jessica,

Joseph,

and

Mary-Catherine

ACKNOWLEDGMENTS

With a grateful heart to my family and friends, especially my parents, Eugene Joseph and Alexandra Mary Cooper; and my brothers and sisters, Alice Jean, Gene, Gary, Barbara, Tim, Michael, and David—I am eternally indebted. I am deeply grateful to St. John Paul II for his inspiration, blessings, and guidance in my life, especially as I wrote this book.

My children—Justin, Chaldea, Jessica, Joseph, and Mary-Catherine—I love you! My husband, David, the wind beneath my wings, thank you for your love and continued support.

My special thanks goes to Robert Hamma, Thomas Grady, and the wonderful, diligent team at Ave Maria Press for their partnership in getting this book out to you.

INTRODUCTION

The Church in her infinite wisdom provides an excellent opportunity for the faithful to grow spiritually and transform their hearts and souls during the penitential season of Lent. With God's saving grace and our own faithful efforts in prayer, fasting, and almsgiving, we can use this time of year wisely to grow deeper in holiness and please God, all while growing closer as a family, too.

St. John Paul II, so beloved to countless people, is an exceptional spiritual guide for your family's Lenten journey. The insightful pontiff reminds us about our Christian responsibility to embrace the forty days of Lent with a greater awareness and attentiveness to the holy season. He encouraged the faithful to observe Lent with great fervor, reliving it with Jesus:

> *"O that today you would hear his voice: harden not your hearts."*
>
> This invitation echoes in our souls as today, Ash Wednesday, we begin our Lenten journey. It will lead to the Easter Triduum, the living memorial of the Lord's passion, death, and resurrection, the central mystery of our salvation.
>
> The holy season of Lent, which has always held deep meaning for the Christian people, recalls ancient biblical events such as the forty days of the universal flood, a prelude to the covenant that God made with Noah; Israel's forty-year pilgrimage through the desert to the promised land; the forty days that Moses remained on Mount Sinai, where he received the tablets of the Law from Yahweh.
>
> In particular, the Lenten season invites us to relive with Jesus the forty days that he spent praying and fasting in the wilderness before beginning his public mission, which culminated on Calvary in the sacrifice of the Cross, the definitive victory over death. (General Audience, February 28, 2001)

Each day, Christian parents have opportunities even amid the busyness of their lives to guide their children toward heaven and its rewards. Called by God to be first and foremost educators, parents can and should do their very best to help mold their children's consciences and souls through their continual example of love and forgiveness, by practicing the virtues, and by creating a loving atmosphere of family prayer in the heart of their home—their domestic church.

Lent is a season meant to transform hearts and souls. This book will provide and encourage a daily occurrence of family prayer and communication as you move through Lent together. By following the suggestions regarding how your family can apply St. John Paul II's wisdom to your lives, you will participate more fully with the rhythm of the Church regarding Lenten prayer, fasting, and almsgiving.

You can choose morning or evening (or hopefully both) to gather with your brood. Your time will be well spent reflecting on St. John Paul II's life and wisdom, as well as the great traditions of Holy Mother Church.

To use this book, simply gather your family and move page by page, day by day, forging your way through Lent. You will see that there are no entries for Saturdays of Lent. I suggest that you use the Sunday prayers and activities throughout the weekend. You can come together morning or evening at your kitchen table, around a prayer table, or wherever you feel most comfortable when praying as a family in your domestic church. Make it special—for example, light a prayer candle if you wish.

St. John Paul II's Inspiration: Each day a quote from St. John Paul II begins the page and sets the tone, in a sense, for the Lenten day.

Parent Reflection: You will be given some points to ponder in this section each day. Some of it will be for you and some for your children.

Family Prayer: There are two opportunities for prayer during each day of meditations—one at the beginning and one at the end. Feel free to elaborate and adapt to suit your family's needs.

A Story from St. John Paul II's Life: This book will highlight notable parts of St. John Paul II's life. This part can be read by an older child or a parent.

Fasting: Each day, "fasting" suggestions will be made to help guide you (the parent) and your children about what to fast from. The fasting will not only be from certain foods, but more often from bad habits or enjoyable activities. Feel free to adapt the suggestions to what works best for your family.

Ash Wednesday and Good Friday are days of fasting and abstinence. Church law requires that no meat be eaten on these days by Catholics fourteen years and older. People with medical conditions and pregnant or nursing mothers are exempt from fasting and abstinence. Catholics from the age of eighteen through fifty-nine must fast on these days by only having one full meatless meal and two smaller meatless and penitential meals. The two small meals together should not equal a full meal.

Almsgiving: Each day "almsgiving" suggestions are provided to help with ideas to accomplish acts of love as a family or individually.

Prayer: Each day you will be given a simple yet poignant thought to think and pray about throughout the day.

May your family receive many rich blessings as you pray, fast, and give alms together and journey toward heaven and its rewards throughout this Lenten season.

ASH WEDNESDAY

"Remember, you are dust and to dust you will return." The traditional rite of distributing ashes, which is repeated today, is always very eloquent, and the words accompanying it are expressive. In its simplicity, it suggests the transitory nature of earthly life: everything passes and is destined to die. We are wayfarers in this world, wayfarers who must never forget their true and final destination: heaven. For, though we are dust and destined to become dust, nevertheless not all will come to an end. Man, created in the image and likeness of God, is destined for eternal life. In dying on the Cross, Jesus opened the way for every human being.

The entire Ash Wednesday liturgy helps us to focus on this fundamental truth of faith and spurs us to undertake a resolute journey of personal renewal. We must change our way of thinking and acting, set our gaze firmly on the face of Christ crucified and make his Gospel our daily rule of life. *"Turn away from sin and be faithful to the Gospel"*: let this be our Lenten program, as we enter an atmosphere of prayerful listening to the Spirit.

—*General Audience, February 28, 2001*

Parent Reflection

Today is a special day because you are embarking on your Lenten journey. We are fortunate to be reminded by our Church that we are entering a very distinctive time within the Church cycle in which we can commit ourselves to prayer, fasting, and almsgiving to please God and to grow in holiness. Today, when you call the family together to begin your Lenten observance, explain to the children that we try to do three things each day during Lent. First, we give up something, and we call this fasting. Second, we give or share something with others—help, possessions, or money. This is called almsgiving. Finally, we pray more. As Catholics, all three of these things should be a certain part of our daily lives, but during the season of Lent, we focus on them more intensely.

Ask the children if they would like to *give up* something for Lent or if they want to *do something* special to please Jesus. Take time today to help them decide and to formulate their Lenten resolutions. You can share with them what you plan to do or give up as well. Help the children write down their resolutions. They can refer to their notes each day throughout Lent. You might want to hang them on the refrigerator, their bedroom door, a bulletin board, or wherever they can be reminded easily.

St. John Paul II's reflection above on the words we will hear today when receiving our ashes—"Remember, you are dust and to dust you will return"—reminds us that these words should cause us to pause and ponder our need to turn away from sin and seek what Jesus wants us to do. In doing so, however, we can hang on to hope, knowing that "in dying on the Cross, Jesus opened the way for every human being."

Family Prayer

All make the Sign of the Cross.

> *Parent:* Dear Jesus, please help us resist getting caught up with the daily worries of life on earth. Help us turn to you in all things, confident that you have opened heaven for all of us to enjoy with you one day. Now let us listen to these words of St. John Paul II.

A parent or child reads the opening quotation aloud.

> *All:* Blessed Mother Mary, bring us closer to your Son, Jesus.

> St. John Paul II, please pray for us. Amen.

A Story from St. John Paul II's Life

St. John Paul II was born as Karol Jozef Wojtyla on May 18, 1920, in the small, ancient town of Wadowice, Poland, about fifty kilometers from Krakow. Karol was the youngest of the three children born to parents Karol Wojtyla (an administrative officer in the Polish army) and Emilia Kaczorowska (a former schoolteacher). Karol's older sister, Olga, had died before he was born.

Karol was baptized on June 20, 1920, by Fr. Franciszek Zak in the parish church of Wadowice. He made his First Holy Communion when he was nine years old and his Confirmation at age eighteen.

Fasting

Discuss with your children what they can offer to God as a sacrifice during Lent. They might choose to give up a favorite video game, dessert, candy, a TV show, or a certain amount of time on the Internet. Decide what you can do as a family, too.

Almsgiving

John Paul II's words above—"We must change our way of thinking and acting, set our gaze firmly on the face of Christ crucified and make his Gospel our daily rule of life"—should inspire us to change for the better. Today, give some time (ten or fifteen minutes) to God. Think about your life and the direction it is headed. Encourage the children to try to ponder how they can serve God better, too.

Prayer

Today's Intention: Let's pray that we may think about our lives and make the necessary changes so that we are pleasing God, not ourselves.

Closing Prayer: Dear Jesus, we are thankful for the opportunity to come together as a family to pray to you. Please grant us the graces we need.

All pray the Our Father, Hail Mary, and Glory Be.

All through the Day: Jesus wants me to focus on the Gospel and not on the distorted messages of the culture.

THURSDAY AFTER ASH WEDNESDAY

"Watch and pray that you may not enter into temptation; the spirit indeed is willing, but the flesh is weak" (Mt 26:41). Let us be guided by these words of the Lord in a committed effort of conversion and spiritual renewal. In daily life, there is a risk of being absorbed in material concerns and interests. Lent is an appropriate time for a reawakening of genuine faith. . . .The means available to us are the same as always, but we must use them more intensely in these weeks: prayer, fasting, and penance, as well as almsgiving, that is, the sharing of what we have with the needy.

—*General Audience, February 28, 2001*

Parent Reflection

Family life is busy. We know all too well that if we let our guard down we can become lackadaisical. St. John Paul II calls us to put a much greater effort into our prayer lives during Lent. He reminds us of the "risk of being absorbed in material concerns and interests." We must always seek to come closer to Jesus and not try to take an easy way out. Likewise, we must guide our children on the narrow path and protect them from an ungodly culture. Make this Lenten season really count!

Family Prayer

All make the Sign of the Cross.

Parent: Dear Jesus, you know how hard it is to get through our daily concerns and know what is right and good. Please give us your light. Keep our family together in prayer and draw us ever closer to you. Now let us listen to these words of St. John Paul II.

A parent or child reads the opening quotation aloud.

All: Blessed Mother Mary, bring us closer to your Son, Jesus.

St. John Paul II, please pray for us. Amen.

A Story from St. John Paul II's Life

Karol's mother Emilia encouraged a vocation in her son by constructing a small altar in his room. His mother had been sickly all of her life and became seriously ill when Karol was eight years old. She was bedridden for some time and then died one day while he was at school. Karol's teacher had to break the news to him, and he quietly said, "It was God's will."

Deep sadness would visit the family again three years later when Karol's older brother, Edmund, who was a physician, died from scarlet fever.

Fasting

Today, fast from discouragement. If you or the kids feel drawn to discouragement, offer up a hopeful prayer. "Lord, help me. I am weak and you are strong. I love you, Jesus."

Almsgiving

Have the children draw a picture or make a card for someone they know who lives alone and try to deliver it soon.

Prayer

Today's Intention: Let's pray for all who live alone: shut-ins, the elderly, even priests alone in rectories.

Closing Prayer: Dear Jesus, please come to the aid of all who are alone and all who are sad to be alone. Please use our prayers and good works to bring them good cheer.

All pray the Our Father, Hail Mary, and Glory Be.

All through the Day: Jesus wants me to think of the lonely and help them in some way.

FRIDAY AFTER ASH WEDNESDAY

"Watch and pray." If Christ's command applies to all times, it seems more eloquent and forceful at the start of Lent. Let us accept it with humble docility. Let us prepare to carry it out in practical acts of conversion and reconciliation with our brethren. Only in this way can faith be reinvigorated, hope be strengthened, and love become the way of life that distinguishes the believer.

—*General Audience, February 28, 2001*

Parent Reflection

Our Church teaches us to "watch and pray." What does that mean in your life right now? Take some time to ponder that today. Talk to the kids about making time in their lives to pray. Help them understand that praying is a wonderful conversation with God. Let them know that God is always waiting for them to reach up to him in prayer. He loves each one of them as a loving Father and loves when your family takes the time to come together in prayer to him.

Family Prayer

All make the Sign of the Cross.

Parent: Dear Jesus, help us seek you in all things. Guide us to reconcile with anyone we might be at odds with, knowing this will please you. Now let us listen to these words of St. John Paul II.

A parent or child reads the opening quotation aloud.

All: Blessed Mother Mary, bring us closer to your Son, Jesus.

St. John Paul II, please pray for us. Amen.

A Story from St. John Paul II's Life

After Edmund died, it was just Karol and his father who remained. They lived in a second-floor apartment at 7 Koscielna Street, a stone house near a bar and café where they would eat their main meals. Each morning, the two would attend Mass together. In the evening after work and school, they would often take a walk and talk about the day.

Karol senior was very devout and raised young Karol with a military-like discipline, the style he was accustomed to. He taught his son German and fostered a love for Polish literature in him. Karol's father was also thrifty and creative and made young Karol's clothing from old uniforms, utilizing his tailoring skills.

Fasting

Today, fast from arguing. Tell the kids that they must not argue. If they feel drawn to arguing, they should stop and pray, "Jesus, help me to be good."

Almsgiving

Today is a good day to give a sincere smile away to someone who has been giving you trouble. Encourage the kids to smile at everyone today and to try to give away their best smile to someone who might not expect it.

Prayer

Today's Intention: Let's pray for all those who don't believe in God.

Closing Prayer: Dear Jesus, help our family be a loving example to others so that they will be drawn to you.

All pray the Our Father, Hail Mary, and Glory Be.

All through the Day: Jesus wants me to spread his love to others.

FIRST SUNDAY OF LENT

At the start of Lent, it is important to prepare our spirit to receive abundantly the gift of divine mercy. The Word of God warns us to repent and believe in the Gospel, and the Church indicates that prayer, penance, fasting, and generous aid to our brethren are the means to enter into the atmosphere of authentic interior and community renewal. In this way, we can experience the superabundant love of the heavenly Father, given in fullness to all humanity in the paschal mystery. We can say that Lent is the time of a particular concern on God's part to pardon and forgive our sins: it is the time of reconciliation. For this reason, it is a most appropriate time for the fruitful reception of the sacrament of Penance.

—General Audience, February 17, 1999

Parent Reflection

Today is the First Sunday of Lent. The gospels in the Church's three-year cycle of readings focus on Jesus' temptation by the devil in the desert (Mt 4:1–11, Mk 1:12–15, Lk 4:1–13). The devil tried to persuade Jesus to bow down to him, but Jesus would not.

You are already a few days into your Lenten journey. St. John Paul II suggests in his words above to prepare your spirit to receive the gift of divine mercy. Have you given thought to preparing your heart this Lent? The words above tell us that when we "repent and believe in the Gospel" and pray, fast, and give alms, we "enter into the atmosphere of authentic interior and community renewal." Schedule a time for the family to go to confession very soon.

Family Prayer

All make the Sign of the Cross.

> *Parent:* Dear Jesus, we are sorry for all of our sins and shortcomings. We want to be better. We want to serve one another more lovingly. With your grace, we will. Now let us listen to these words of St. John Paul II.

A parent or child reads the opening quotation aloud.

> *All:* Blessed Mother Mary, bring us closer to your Son, Jesus.
>
> St. John Paul II, please pray for us. Amen.

A Story from St. John Paul II's Life

Karol was very well-rounded in his studies and activities. He received a classical education at the state-run boys' school he attended in his town. Latin and Greek were at the core of his studies. As a young man, he got involved in a society called the Solidarity of Mary, which fostered a devotion to the Blessed Mother. He was required to attend a cadet camp to study military preparedness. His love for the theater blossomed at this time.

Fasting

Today, fast from gossip. If you or the children feel a need to talk about someone, stop and say a prayer instead.

Almsgiving

Since today is Sunday—a family day—schedule a time to sit down together and talk about ways to bring love to someone this week. Some ideas might be to make a dessert or greeting card to bring to a shut-in, to offer to help an elderly neighbor with a chore, or to visit someone who would appreciate some company.

Prayer

> *Today's Intention:* Let's pray for all orphans of the world, that they will be blessed with a home soon.
>
> *Closing Prayer:* Dear Jesus, please take care of the orphans. Please bring them comfort and love.
>
> *All pray the Our Father, Hail Mary, and Glory Be.*
>
> *All through the Day:* God wants me to confess my sins and stay close to him in prayer.

MONDAY, FIRST WEEK OF LENT

The beginning of the season of Lent invites us to turn to God our Father with great trust in his mercy and love.

—*General Audience, February 17, 1999*

Parent Reflection

As parents we are called each day to trust God with our lives and our circumstances. Some days it's easier than others. The season of Lent beckons us to trust in God's mercy and love in an even deeper way. Talk to the children today about trusting in God. Ask them what they can do to trust him more. Ponder it with them and give them some ideas. Then try to apply the ideas to your lives.

Family Prayer

All make the Sign of the Cross.

> *Parent:* Dear Jesus, help us surrender our hearts to you today. Now let us listen to these words of St. John Paul II.

A parent or child reads the opening quotation aloud.

> *All:* Blessed Mother Mary, bring us closer to your Son, Jesus.

St. John Paul II, please pray for us. Amen.

A Story from St. John Paul II's Life

Karol excelled in his studies and was a very fine student. In addition to his interest in learning and acting, he became an athlete. He played soccer and practiced with a ball his father made for him out of rags. He became a superb goalie. He also swam in nearby rivers in the springtime, when they were flowing from the melted snow. He loved to kayak, ski, climb mountains, hike, and camp out in the wilderness.

Karol graduated from his secondary school, Marcin Wadowita high school, in 1938 as valedictorian.

Fasting

Today, fast from wasting time or from procrastination. God wants you to put your time to good use and not to be slothful. Think with the children about how to structure your days to be more pleasing to God.

Almsgiving

Tell a special story today. Take a few minutes and recall a special moment when someone helped you and it meant a lot to you. Share it with a family member today. You can do this at the dinner table tonight and share together.

Prayer

> *Today's Intention:* Let's pray for all who are sick and suffering.
>
> *Closing Prayer:* Dear Jesus, look kindly upon all who suffer in some way. Give us the time and ability to help them.
>
> *All pray the Our Father, Hail Mary, and Glory Be.*
>
> *All through the Day:* Jesus, I trust in you.

So endeavor to penetrate the meaning of Christ's poverty if you want to be rich! Seek to penetrate the meaning of his weakness if you want to obtain salvation! Seek to penetrate the meaning of his crucifixion if you do not want to be ashamed of it; the meaning of his wounds, if you want yours to heal; the meaning of his death, if you want to gain eternal life; and the meaning of his burial, if you want to find the Resurrection.

—*General Audience, June 2, 2004*

Parent Reflection

There is so much to accomplish even in the course of one day, and we sometimes fly from one activity to the next worrying that we won't get everything done. It's only natural to want to take care of our responsibilities. But we should know that we are also responsible for taking care of our spiritual lives and those of our children, too. Try to read St. John Paul II's words above several times today. There is so much meaning in them to ponder. Help the children understand them. Perhaps you can discuss them for a few minutes at dinner tonight.

Family Prayer

All make the Sign of the Cross.

> *Parent*: Dear Jesus, help us devote more time to you and to learning more about our faith. Now let us listen to these words of St. John Paul II.

A parent or child reads the opening quotation aloud.

> *All*: Blessed Mother Mary, bring us closer to your Son, Jesus.

> St. John Paul II, please pray for us. Amen.

A Story from St. John Paul II's Life

In 1938, after he graduated from high school, Karol and his father moved to nearby Krakow, which was considered to be the cultural and intellectual center of Poland. There Karol enrolled in the Jagiellonian University to study literature and philosophy. In addition, he enrolled in a school for drama to pursue his love of the stage. Karol further developed his acting abilities, and he began to sing and write poetry.

Fasting

Today, fast from worrying. Try to give all of your problems and concerns to God. If helpful, you and the kids can write them down on paper and say a prayer. Then rip up the paper and throw it away. Trust God with all of it.

Almsgiving

Since St. John Paul II loved acting, give some time to creating a short, simple skit the kids can act out that will show trust in God. Or, choose an appropriate play or movie to discuss at the dinner table tonight.

Prayer

Today's Intention: Let's pray for all students and those aspiring to further studies.

Closing Prayer: Dear Jesus, help us realize our vocation. Help us always to seek your will in our lives.

All pray the Our Father, Hail Mary, and Glory Be.

All through the Day: God wants me to share my time, talents, and treasures with others.

WEDNESDAY, FIRST WEEK OF LENT

Just as Christ once said to Peter, so to everyone he repeats: *Duc in altum!* [Put out into the deep!] He invites us to put out into the deep and to venture undaunted into the sea of life, trusting in the constant support of Mary, Mother of God, and in the intercession of the Apostles Peter and Paul, who with their blood made the early Church fertile.

—*General Audience, June 30, 2004*

Parent Reflection

So much of our parenting requires a deep trust in God. When we welcome new life into our lives, we in essence "put out into the deep" as St. John Paul II mentions in his words above. There are no guarantees in raising our families. We trust, pray, and do the best we can to guide our little saints to heaven. Let's remember to call upon Mother Mary as St. John Paul II suggests. She will continually support us in our parenting. Take some time today to seek Mother Mary in your prayers and to talk to the children about their Mother in heaven.

Family Prayer

All make the Sign of the Cross.

> *Parent:* Dear Jesus, help us trust in you more with our daily lives. Now let us listen to these words of St. John Paul II.

A parent or child reads the opening quotation aloud.

> *All:* Blessed Mother Mary, bring us closer to your Son, Jesus.

> St. John Paul II, please pray for us. Amen.

A Story from St. John Paul II's Life

In 1939, Germany invaded Poland, and the Nazi occupation forces closed the university where Karol was attending. On the morning of the invasion, Karol was in the cathedral and could hear the warning sirens and then the sounds of gunfire and exploding bombs dropped by Luftwaffe aircraft. As the invasion was set in motion, Karol immediately ran for home. The next six years would be heartrending and tragic for Poland. Later, on the fiftieth anniversary of the end of the war, Pope John Paul II said the Nazi occupation was a period of "fear, violence, extreme poverty, death, tragic experiences of painful separation, endured in the absence of all security and freedom; recurring traumas brought about by the incessant bloodshed" (Message, May 8, 1995).

Fasting

Today, fast from all negativity. Remind the children to try their best to be positive no matter how the day unfolds.

Almsgiving

Give away time today. Help someone with a chore, call someone who might be lonely, or give Jesus more of your time in prayer today. Encourage the kids to do the same.

Prayer

Today's Intention: Let's pray for all areas of conflict and war, that they may experience God's peace.

Closing Prayer: Dear Jesus, bring us your peace.

All pray the Our Father, Hail Mary, and Glory Be.

All through the Day: Jesus wants me to reach out in love.

THURSDAY, FIRST WEEK OF LENT

Dear brothers and sisters, knowing that our reconciliation with God takes place through authentic conversion, let us begin our Lenten pilgrimage with our eyes fixed on Christ, our only Redeemer.

—*General Audience, February 17, 1999*

Parent Reflection

There are many opportunities even in the course of one day to offer forgiveness to another or to say, "I'm sorry." By humbling ourselves, we allow God to work on our hearts—to convert us—and to bring us closer to him. It can be tough sometimes, but don't let pride get in the way of authentic conversion. Humble yourself and offer your heart to your family through love and forgiveness. Then you can expect miracles!

Family Prayer

All make the Sign of the Cross.

Parent: Dear Jesus, take our hearts and make them more like yours. Now let us listen to these words of St. John Paul II.

A parent or child reads the opening quotation aloud.

All: Blessed Mother Mary, bring us closer to your Son, Jesus.

St. John Paul II, please pray for us. Amen.

A Story from St. John Paul II's Life

Karol was forced to stop his formal education at the university because it was closed down by the Nazis. He had to earn a living as a laborer in a limestone quarry from 1940 to 1944 and then in a chemical factory in Solvay so as to avoid being deported to Germany or being imprisoned or even executed.

It was a harsh repression. The Nazis were after Jews, priests, and intellectuals. Some of Karol's Jewish friends had fled Poland. The Catholic clergy had no other choice but to go underground. Though careful, Karol did not want to be intimidated by the Nazis and was actively involved in leading a secret Catholic youth group.

Fasting

Today, fast from self-centeredness. Tell the children to think of others more than their own desires.

Almsgiving

Ask the children to think about giving away a toy or game to the needy. Then decide as a family where you can donate it.

Prayer

Today's Intention: Let's pray for the unfortunate and homeless.

Closing Prayer: Dear Jesus, look kindly upon the homeless. Please bring others to them to offer help and hope.

All pray the Our Father, Hail Mary, and Glory Be.

All through the Day: I need to focus more on the needs of others.

FRIDAY, FIRST WEEK OF LENT

So it is that our poor humanity is snatched from the deviating, twisted paths of evil and brought back to "righteousness," that is, to the beautiful plan of God. . . . "By his wounds you have been healed." Here we see how dearly Christ paid to obtain our healing!

—*General Audience, September 22, 2004*

Parent Reflection

Our days are usually filled to the brim. We hit the ground running, eager to accomplish all we need to do. It might seem that there is not enough time to get it all done, and we sigh or lament that we didn't pray enough. Let's at least take some time today to meditate on our Lord's passion and death. As St. John Paul II said in his words above, Christ paid dearly to obtain our healing. Talk to the kids today about making a special effort to be more thankful to God for their blessings. Help them recognize the blessings that surround them.

Family Prayer

All make the Sign of the Cross.

Parent: Dear Jesus, you give us so many blessings for which we are thankful. We are sorry for not thanking you enough. Now let us listen to these words of St. John Paul II.

A parent or child reads the opening quotation aloud.

All: Blessed Mother Mary, bring us closer to your Son, Jesus.

St. John Paul II, please pray for us. Amen.

A Story from St. John Paul II's Life

In 1941, Karol's father died of a heart attack. It was after his father's death that Karol began to clearly hear a calling to the priesthood. He described his vocation as "an inner fact of unquestionable and absolute clarity. The following year, in the autumn, I knew that I was called."[1] Karol began courses in a secret seminary that was established in a church in Krakow and run by Cardinal Adam Stefan Sapieha, archbishop of Krakow. During this time, Karol was also involved in theater and was one of the founders of the clandestine "Rhapsodic Theater."

Fasting

Today, fast from taking things for granted. Pause and ponder your many blessings and thank God for them. Set aside a time to help the children do the same.

Almsgiving

Encourage the kids to make an honest list of ten blessings in their lives. The younger ones may draw them, and the older ones can write them down. Save the drawings and lists and have the kids read them and ponder them during Holy Week.

Prayer

Today's Intention: Let's pray for all families of the world, in every shape and size.

Closing Prayer: Dear Jesus, thank you for the gift of our family and for suffering so intensely to open the gates of heaven for us.

All pray the Our Father, Hail Mary, and Glory Be.

All through the Day: I have so much for which to give thanks to God. I should strive to thank God more often.

SECOND SUNDAY OF LENT

St. Cyril of Jerusalem (fourth century) uses Psalm 32 [31] to teach catechumens of the profound renewal of Baptism, a radical purification from all sin. Using the words of the Psalmist, he too exalts divine mercy. We end our catechesis with his words: "God is merciful and is not stingy in granting forgiveness. . . . The mountain of your sins will not rise above the greatness of God's mercy, the depth of your wounds will not overcome the skillfulness of the 'most high' Doctor: on condition that you abandon yourself to him with trust. Make known your evil to the Doctor, and address him with the words of the prophet David: 'I will confess to the Lord the sin that is always before me.' In this way, these words will follow: 'You have forgiven the ungodliness of my heart.'"

—*General Audience, May 19, 2004*

Parent Reflection

Today is the Second Sunday of Lent. The gospels in the Church's three-year cycle of readings speak about the transfiguration of Jesus (Mt 17:1–9, Mk 9:2–10, Lk 9:28–36). Peter, James, and John were taken up on a high mountain by Jesus, who revealed his glory to them. Jesus' face and clothes suddenly dazzled a pure, radiant white. A voice spoke from a cloud, "This is my beloved Son, with whom I am well pleased; listen to him" (Mt 17:5). This encounter frightened the disciples, who fell down. Jesus comforted them and asked them not to reveal what they saw to anyone until he rose from the dead. The experience gave the disciples strength for the journey ahead. Ask God for strength for your journey.

St. John Paul II reminds us, "God is merciful and is not stingy in granting forgiveness." He awaits our communication with him; he wants our repentant hearts. How many times do we hold a grudge or are slow to forgive? Are we stingy in granting forgiveness to those who have harmed us in some way? Even if someone has not asked for our forgiveness, we can forgive them and pray for them. That's what our Lord is calling us to do. Opportunities for forgiveness and mercy truly exist in the heart of your home. Will you look for them today? Encourage the kids to forgive one another, emphasizing the importance of practicing the virtues.

Family Prayer

All make the Sign of the Cross.

Parent: Dear Jesus, help our family grow in holiness. Now let us listen to these words of St. John Paul II.

A parent or child reads the opening quotation aloud.

All: Blessed Mother Mary, bring us closer to your Son, Jesus.

St. John Paul II, please pray for us. Amen.

A Story from St. John Paul II's Life

Karol was among the ten candidates chosen for the first class of priests to be ordained through the clandestine seminary in Krakow. After the Second World War, the seminary reopened and Karol was able to continue studies there as well as with the faculty of theology of the Jagiellonian University, also in Krakow. On November 1, 1946, Karol was ordained to the priesthood by Cardinal Adam Stefan Sapieha in a small, private chapel.

Fasting

Today, fast from any quarreling. Encourage the family to be virtuous today and always.

Almsgiving

Ask the children to consider how they might be an instrument of God's peace today.

Prayer

Today's Intention: Let's pray for peace in the world.

Closing Prayer: Dear Jesus, please help us help one another in our family, choosing to put others before ourselves.

All pray the Our Father, Hail Mary, and Glory Be.

All through the Day: My prayers and acts of love please God and help others.

MONDAY, SECOND WEEK OF LENT

The embrace of reconciliation between the Father and all sinful humanity took place on Calvary. May the Crucifix, sign of the love of Christ who sacrificed himself for our salvation, instill in the hearts of every man and woman of our time that same trust which prompted the prodigal son to say: "I will arise and go to my father, and I will say to him, 'Father, I have sinned.'" He received the gift of forgiveness and joy.

—*General Audience, February 17, 1999*

Parent Reflection

How many times do we pass by a crucifix or see it on our Rosary or at church and not pause to ponder the deep meaning in Christ's sacrifice for us—for our salvation? St. John Paul II tells us in his words above that the crucifix is a sign of God's love and can prompt us to seek reconciliation. Talk to the children about the great gifts of reconciliation and forgiveness. Ask them to think about the times they have not lived up to God's expectations of them and your expectations, too. Encourage them to ask for forgiveness from one another and also from God. Schedule a time for confession soon if you haven't done so yet.

Family Prayer

All make the Sign of the Cross.

> *Parent:* Dear Jesus, please forgive us of our sins. Give us strength and courage to rise above what the culture dictates to us and answer to you instead. Now let us listen to these words of St. John Paul II.

A parent or child reads the opening quotation aloud.

> *All:* Blessed Mother Mary, bring us closer to your Son, Jesus.

St. John Paul II, please pray for us. Amen.

A Story from St. John Paul II's Life

Shortly after Karol Wojtyla was ordained, he was sent to a poor rural parish. Later he was assigned to a thriving parish, St. Florian's in Krakow, where university students attended Mass. While he was there, the Catholic Church came under attack again, this time by the Soviets. Cardinal Sapieha then sent Fr. Wojtyla to Rome to work under the guidance of the French Dominican Fr. Reginald Garrigou-Lagrange. Fr. Wojtyla worked on his studies and earned his doctorate in theology in 1948. His thesis was based on the theme of faith in the writings of St. John of the Cross.

Fasting

Today, fast from judging. If you are tempted to judge a particular situation or person, keep quiet and take it to prayer. Encourage the kids to do this as well.

Almsgiving

Have the children (with your help) write a note of reconciliation to a family member or friend.

Prayer

Today's Intention: Let's pray for the souls in purgatory.

Closing Prayer: Dear Jesus, we love you and are sorry for ever having offended you. Please forgive us of our sins.

All pray the Our Father, Hail Mary, and Glory Be.

All through the Day: Jesus loves me with an infinite and merciful love.

TUESDAY, SECOND WEEK OF LENT

First of all, there is he, Christ, who sets out on the inexorable journey of the Passion without protesting against the injustice and violence, without recrimination or outbursts, but entrusting himself and his sorrowful experience "to him who judges justly" (1 Pt 2:23). This act of pure and total trust was to be sealed on the Cross with his famous last words, cried with a loud voice as his supreme abandonment to the will of the Father: "Father, into your hands I commit my spirit!" (Lk 23:46; cf. Ps 31:6).

—*General Audience, September 22, 2004*

Parent Reflection

We don't like to be wronged. We even fight against injustices toward others. But sometimes no matter what we do, our lives are spattered with insults and unjust acts against us. Can you be mindful, even in the smallest instances, of lifting up in prayer the culprits in your life? Take some time today to ponder who they are and maybe even why you think they do what they do. Do they need help? Are they hurting? They certainly need your prayers. Endeavor to pray for those who harm you or try to harm you in some way. Encourage the children to pray an Our Father for their "enemies" and to focus on the words "forgive us our trespasses *as we forgive* those who trespass against us."

Family Prayer

All make the Sign of the Cross.

Parent: Dear Jesus, forgive us and help us forgive others. Now let us listen to these words of St. John Paul II.

A parent or child reads the opening quotation aloud.

All: Blessed Mother Mary, bring us closer to your Son, Jesus.

St. John Paul II, please pray for us. Amen.

A Story from St. John Paul II's Life

In 1948, Fr. Wojtyla returned to his homeland and became a vicar to many parishes in Krakow. He also acted as chaplain to the university students. In 1951, he again took up studies in theology and philosophy. A couple of years later, in 1953, Fr. Wojtyla defended his thesis on the importance of the work of the German philosopher Max Scheler at Lublin Catholic University.

Fasting

Today, fast from wasting time. Encourage the children to have a plan for their free time. Have them do something constructive and positive.

Almsgiving

Give some time away today. Have everyone write a little note to a family member with a promise of a special prayer or deed for them.

Prayer

Today's Intention: Let's pray for bullies, asking God to help them so they won't hurt others.

Closing Prayer: Dear Jesus, thank you for blessing us with our faith in you.

All pray the Our Father, Hail Mary, and Glory Be.

All through the Day: I will try to be more mindful of the needs around me and less focused on myself.

In being born of the Virgin Mary, he became our brother. So it is that he can stand beside us, share in our pain and bear our wickedness, "our sins" (1 Pt 2:24). But he is also and always the Son of God, and his solidarity with us becomes radically transforming, liberating, expiatory, and salvific.

—*General Audience, September 22, 2004*

Parent Reflection

The *Catechism of the Catholic Church* tells us, "The Christian home is the place where children receive the first proclamation of the faith. For this reason the family home is rightly called 'the domestic church,' a community of grace and prayer, a school of human virtues, and of Christian charity" (CCC 1666). Your home might not seem like a church when things are chaotic, when there is sibling rivalry or growing pains going on, or teenage angst is flaring up. But it indeed is a little church comprised of people growing together in holiness as they love one another during the give and take of family living.

Family Prayer

All make the Sign of the Cross.

> *Parent*: Dear Jesus, thank you for our family. Please help us grow in holiness. Now let us listen to these words of St. John Paul II.

A parent or child reads the opening quotation aloud.

> *All*: Blessed Mother Mary, bring us closer to your Son, Jesus.

St. John Paul II, please pray for us. Amen.

A Story from St. John Paul II's Life

God's plans for Karol Wojtyla were constantly unfolding, and though he didn't know it, God was leading him to become the pope. On July 4, 1958, Pope Pius XII appointed Fr. Wojtyla auxiliary bishop of

Krakow. He was consecrated on September 28, 1958, by Archbishop Eugeniusz Baziak in Wawel Cathedral in Krakow. Bishop Wojtyla was constantly moving forward by God's design. Less than six years later, on January 13, 1964, Bishop Wojtyla was appointed archbishop of Krakow by Pope Paul VI.

Fasting

Today, fast from a treat. Encourage the children to do the same.

Almsgiving

Give God extra time in prayer today, and ask the children to say an extra prayer on their own, too.

Prayer

> *Today's Intention*: Let's pray for all of the sick and dying around the world, that they will be given love and healing.
>
> *Closing Prayer*: Dear Jesus, help us spread your love everywhere we go.
>
> *All pray the Our Father, Hail Mary, and Glory Be.*
>
> *All through the Day*: God is counting on me to love others.

THURSDAY, SECOND WEEK OF LENT

Lent helps Christians to enter more deeply into this "mystery hidden for ages" (Eph 3:9): it leads them to come face to face with the word of the living God and urges them to give up their own selfishness in order to receive the saving activity of the Holy Spirit.

—Message for Lent 2000

Parent Reflection

St. John Paul II reminds us in his words above that the special season of Lent calls us to go deeper into the mystery of God. God calls us to pray, fast, and give alms so that we can allow the Holy Spirit to inspire us—and thereby inspire others through our lives of love. Ponder some ways you can encourage the family to delve deeper into Lent today. Can you read a story about a saint or a passage from the *Catechism* at the dinner table tonight? Start a conversation about the Faith.

Family Prayer

All make the Sign of the Cross.

> *Parent*: Dear Jesus, we want to come closer to you. We want to help bring others closer, too. Now let us listen to these words of St. John Paul II.

A parent or child reads the opening quotation aloud.

> *All*: Blessed Mother Mary, bring us closer to your Son, Jesus.

> St. John Paul II, please pray for us. Amen.

A Story from St. John Paul II's Life

It turns out that at the time of the appointment of the new archbishop in Krakow, the Communist officials were concerned about threats to their plans and turned down the first two lists of potential candidates.

But because Bishop Wojtyla seemed more of an intellectual, poet, and academic, and less of a political threat, the Communists accepted him as a candidate to be appointed. Archbishop Wojtyla also served on the papal commission that helped write the encyclical *Humanae Vitae*, which articulated the Church's teaching on birth control. After appointing Wojtyla archbishop of Krakow, Pope Paul VI made him a cardinal on June 26, 1967, a short three years later.

Fasting

Today, fast from boasting. If the kids feel tempted to brag or focus only on themselves, have them pause and give credit to others instead.

Almsgiving

Encourage the children to show God's love to someone who is not expecting it today. Help them with ideas of how they might accomplish this.

Prayer

Today's Intention: Let's pray for all of the unbelievers in the world.

Closing Prayer: Dear Jesus, forgive us of our shortcomings and help us do better tomorrow.

All pray the Our Father, Hail Mary, and Glory Be.

All through the Day: By allowing Jesus to live through me, I can help so many others.

FRIDAY, SECOND WEEK OF LENT

During Lent, everyone—rich and poor—is invited to make Christ's love present through generous works of charity. . . . Our charity is called in a particular way to manifest Christ's love to our brothers and sisters who lack the necessities of life, who suffer hunger, violence, or injustice.

Lent helps Christians to enter more deeply into this "mystery hidden for ages."

—*Message for Lent 2000*

Parent Reflection

Sometimes we feel as if we are out of time. We are so busy raising our families and are often exhausted from doing what we do. How can we possibly take on other works of charity as St. John Paul II speaks about above? First and foremost, we are to take care of our duties in the home. It would be wrong to go off and offer charitable works everywhere but at home. As Mother Teresa always professed, "Love begins at home." So, let's be sure to get our priorities straight, and then devise a way we can help the poor and needy outside the family. Take some time today to plan an act of love and mercy you can perform as a family this weekend or soon.

Family Prayer

All make the Sign of the Cross.

Parent: Dear Jesus, we want to spread your love to others. Now let us listen to these words of St. John Paul II.

A parent or child reads the opening quotation aloud.

All: Blessed Mother Mary, bring us closer to your Son, Jesus.

St. John Paul II, please pray for us. Amen.

A Story from St. John Paul II's Life

Archbishop Wojtyla participated in the Second Vatican Council, which convened four times between 1962 and 1965. He made important contributions to the drafting of the Pastoral Constitution on the Church, *Gaudium et Spes*. He also participated in the first Synod of Bishops after the Council. In 1978, Cardinal Albino Luciani, patriarch of Venice, became Pope John Paul I after just four ballots. However, he died just thirty-three days later. Another pope needed to be elected for the Church. Even though he was only fifty-eight at that time, Archbishop Wojtyla's name kept coming up as a perfect candidate for the next pope.

Fasting

Today, fast from selfishness. We should never be selfish, but today focus on ways to live unselfishly. Encourage the children in this as well.

Almsgiving

Give some extra time in prayer today for the needy and unfortunate. Get together and think of a way to do a loving act as a family this weekend.

Prayer

Today's Intention: Let's pray for the poor of the world.

Closing Prayer: Dear Jesus, help us love others with your love.

All pray the Our Father, Hail Mary, and Glory Be.

All through the Day: Jesus wants to fill my heart with joy to give to others.

THIRD SUNDAY OF LENT

In his *Exposition on Psalm 109*, which he gave during Lent in the year 412, [St Augustine] describes the Psalm as a true prophecy of the divine promises regarding Christ. The famous Father of the Church said: "It was necessary to know the only-begotten Son of God, who was to come among men, to take flesh and become a man through the nature he took on: he was to die, to rise again, and to ascend into Heaven, where he was to sit at the right hand of the Father and fulfill all he had promised among the peoples. . . . All this, therefore, had to be prophesied, had to be foretold, had to be signaled as destined to occur, in order not to give rise to fear by coming like a bolt from the blue, but rather to be anticipated with faith and hope."

—*General Audience, August 18, 2004*

Parent Reflection

Today is the Third Sunday of Lent. The gospels for the Church's three-year cycle of readings, though different each year, all invite us to a conversion of heart and to be mindful of Ash Wednesday's message: "Turn away from sin and be faithful to the Gospel." In one gospel reading, Jesus offers his "living water" to the Samaritan woman (Jn 4:5–42), inviting her to repent and experience a true conversion. In another, Jesus forcefully ejects the money changers in the Temple (Jn 2:13–25); and finally, Jesus gives the example of the barren fig tree (Lk 13:1–9) to explain God's abundant patience with us even when we fail him.

In the words above, both St. Augustine and St. John Paul II tell us we need to get to know Jesus. Prayer really helps in that regard. Prayer, after all, is our conversation with God. Let's ponder today whether our *conversation* with God is one-sided or whether we allow him room to speak to us. If we are spending too much time doing the talking, perhaps it's time to change our prayer habits. There's nothing wrong with spending ample time talking to God, but let's be sure we give him time to speak to our hearts. Let's pause and be silent and do our best to listen to him.

Family Prayer

> *All make the Sign of the Cross.*
>
> > Parent: Dear Jesus, help us get to know you better. Now let us listen to these words of St. John Paul II.
>
> *A parent or child reads the opening quotation aloud.*
>
> > All: Blessed Mother Mary, bring us closer to your Son, Jesus.
>
> St. John Paul II, please pray for us. Amen.

A Story from St. John Paul II's Life

On October 16, 1978, the Conclave of Cardinals elected Cardinal Karol Wojtyla pope. He took the name John Paul II. Many were perplexed, wondering why the new pope was not Italian (he was the first non-Italian pope in four-and-a-half centuries). But the new pope quelled their fears. In perfect Italian the charming Wojtyla said, "I am your new bishop of Rome, called from a distant country. I don't know if I can make myself clear in your—our—Italian language. If I make a mistake, you will correct me." That remarkably good nature and spirit would continue to be a huge part of the young pontiff's trademark.

Fasting

Today, fast from talking too much. Try your best to strive for quiet today and encourage the kids to do the same.

Almsgiving

Give up talking whenever you can today, and take a half hour of silence in the home if possible. Tell the kids that they are to find a quiet place and try to listen to God.

Prayer

Today's Intention: Let's pray for all of our "enemies."

Closing Prayer: Dear Jesus, help us be more mindful of taking time to listen to you and learn about you.

All pray the Our Father, Hail Mary, and Glory Be.

All through the Day: It's not all about me; it's all about God.

Lent is a time for us to seek the gift of the Father's mercy through authentic personal and community renewal. This renewal involves prayer, fasting, and charitable acts, and is most intensely experienced in the Sacrament of Penance. As we look forward to Easter, may our Lenten journey help us to put aside whatever hinders our friendship with God.

—*General Audience, February 17, 1999*

Parent Reflection

You are making your way through Lent with your family. Many of the readings remind us of the penitential aspect of Lent but also of the renewal of heart and reconciliation. If you haven't been to confession as a family yet this Lenten season, try to schedule it today. St. John Paul II explains that when we have sins or failings separating us from God and others, our friendship with God is hindered. Remind the children today about the importance of forgiveness and love.

Family Prayer

All make the Sign of the Cross.

Parent: Dear Jesus, we want to clear our hearts and souls of anything that inhibits us from your friendship. Now let us listen to these words of St. John Paul II.

A parent or child reads the opening quotation aloud.

All: Blessed Mother Mary, bring us closer to your Son, Jesus.

St. John Paul II, please pray for us. Amen.

A Story from St. John Paul II's Life

On October 22, 1978, Pope John Paul II inaugurated his Petrine ministry, becoming the 263rd successor of St. Peter. His pontificate would be one of the longest ever in the Church's history, enduring for twenty-seven years. It was apparent that John Paul II put his whole heart and soul into his position as leader of the Catholic Church. His dedication, love, commitment, and marvelous missionary spirit spoke volumes. He was a beloved man, one who would bring about great changes by God's grace.

Fasting

Today, fast from a bit of comfort—an extra portion of food, a dessert, extra time in the shower, or extra time to sleep. You know what you like and what will make a good sacrifice. Ask the children if they would consider fasting from something, too.

Almsgiving

Give ten minutes or more of your time to someone today when you'd rather be doing something else, and encourage the kids to give time to someone else as well.

Prayer

Today's Intention: Let's pray for those who have no one to pray for them.

Closing Prayer: Dear Jesus, help us grow in holiness in our domestic church.

All pray the Our Father, Hail Mary, and Glory Be.

All through the Day: God grants me grace and wants me to ask for more.

The fruit of such a courageous ascetical journey can only be a greater openness to the needs of our neighbor. Those who love the Lord cannot close their eyes to individuals and peoples who are tried by suffering and poverty. After contemplating the face of the crucified Lord, how can we not recognize him and serve him in those who are suffering and abandoned? Jesus himself, who invites us to stay with him watching and praying, also asks us to love him in our brothers and sisters, remembering that "as you did it to one of the least of these my brethren, you did it to me" (Mt 25:40). The fruit of a Lent intensely lived will thus be a greater and more universal love.

—*General Audience, February 28, 2001*

Parent Reflection

St. John Paul II and Blessed Mother Teresa of Calcutta remind us that God calls us to live the Gospel truth that "as you did it to one of the least of these my brethren, you did it to me" (Mt 25:40). Everything we do and don't do affects others in some way. Do we remember that Jesus lives in all of us and that our Lord asks us to serve Jesus in them? When we do, our Lord is very pleased and hearts are transformed—theirs and ours.

Family Prayer

All make the Sign of the Cross.

Parent: Dear Jesus, we want to serve you more lovingly in our family members, neighbors, and community. Now let us listen to these words of St. John Paul II.

A parent or child reads the opening quotation aloud.

All: Blessed Mother Mary, bring us closer to your Son, Jesus.

St. John Paul II, please pray for us. Amen.

A Story from St. John Paul II's Life

In 1979, Pope John Paul II made his first papal trip to Latin America. Arriving in Mexico City, he observed the millions of Mexicans lined up at the sides of roads all around the city, waiting to catch a glimpse of their *Papa*. Ten thousand people were crammed into the airport proper to watch him descend the steps of the plane to bless them. One admirer adorned the pope's head with a traditional sombrero. He would later receive flowers and kisses from kindhearted children.

He met with the clergy, with nuns, and with the laity. He visited the Polish colony and partook in festivities. Later, he said Mass in the metropolitan cathedral. Afterward, he prayed at the shrine of *La Virgen Morena*, the Virgin of Guadalupe, and was deeply moved. He clearly realized then that God was calling him to be a pilgrim pope[2]— one who would visit many areas of the globe to inspire and ignite faith and to right wrongs. In a sense, he would become a physical presence of the Church among the peoples.

Fasting

Today, fast from technology as best as you can. Encourage everyone to stay off the Internet and to avoid watching TV.

Almsgiving

Give some time to spiritual reading. Set a timer for a half hour and have or help the children read about a life of a saint.

Prayer

> *Today's Intention*: Let's pray for all those in seemingly impossible situations.
>
> *Closing Prayer*: Dear Jesus, please let our prayers bring forth fruits.
>
> *All pray the Our Father, Hail Mary, and Glory Be.*
>
> *All through the Day*: Mother Mary will draw me closer to her Son, Jesus.

He put on our humanity in the womb of the Virgin and was born like a man. . . . It is he who as a lamb was taken away and as a lamb was slaughtered, thereby redeeming us from the slavery of the world. . . . It is he who brought us from slavery to freedom, from darkness to light, from death to life, from oppression to eternal kingship; and he made us a new priesthood and a chosen people forever. . . . It is he, the silent Lamb, the slain Lamb, the Son of Mary, the Lamb without stain. He was seized by the flock, led to his death, slain toward evening, and buried at night.

—*General Audience, March 31, 2004*

Parent Reflection

Jesus knows all about suffering. We often lament or complain about our situations, forgetting that God, the Divine Physician, knows exactly what we need to turn our hearts more fully toward him. Talk to the children today about accepting their circumstances—not with grumbling, but as much as possible with gladness and a grateful heart. Look at your own life and ponder ways you can be more thankful for your circumstances and ways you can share your blessings with others.

Family Prayer

All make the Sign of the Cross.

Parent: Dear Jesus, help us to be more thankful to you. Now let us listen to these words of St. John Paul II.

A parent or child reads the opening quotation aloud.

All: Blessed Mother Mary, bring us closer to your Son, Jesus.

St. John Paul II, please pray for us. Amen.

A Story from St. John Paul II's Life

There were hundreds of thousands of Mexicans who came out to greet Pope John Paul II throughout his entire trip throughout Mexico. The new pontiff was clearly impressed and moved by the faithfulness and piety of the people. He told them that he was delighted to be a pilgrim in a land that loved the Blessed Mother as did his native Poland.

When coming face-to-face with thousands upon thousands of poor people of Cuilapam de Guerrero in Mexico, the new pope addressed them saying that he wanted to be "the voice of those who cannot speak or are silent; the defender of the oppressed, who have the right to effective help, not charity or the crumbs of justice."[3]

In Oaxaca, one of Mexico's most impoverished areas, the barefooted Indians in tattered clothing came out in droves to see the pope, and it moved him profoundly. The pope gave a very emotional speech. He denounced poverty by saying, "It is not Christian to maintain unjust situations."[4] He instructed the people to use spiritual and moral persuasion and not violence to solve the problem of poverty.

Fasting

Today, fast from complaining. When tempted to complain, say, "Jesus, I love you." Ask the children to do the same.

Almsgiving

Help the family make a list of reasons they are thankful. Talk about a way you can give a surprise gift (such as time, a dessert, or a card) to someone in need.

Prayer

Today's Intention: Let's pray for the victims of poverty.

Closing Prayer: Dear Jesus, help us help others. Give us generous hearts.

All pray the Our Father, Hail Mary, and Glory Be.

All through the Day: Jesus gives me everything I need to grow in holiness.

THURSDAY, THIRD WEEK OF LENT

In the end, Christ himself, the slaughtered Lamb, calls to all peoples: "So come, you of all races of men who are ensnared by your sins and receive forgiveness for your sins. Indeed, I am your forgiveness, the Passover of your salvation; I am the Lamb slain for you, I am your redemption, your way, your resurrection, your light, your salvation, and your king. It is I who lead you to the heights of Heaven, I who will show you the Father who exists from eternity, I who will raise you to life with my right hand."

—*General Audience, March 31, 2004*

Parent Reflection

Jesus who suffered and died for us offers us forgiveness of our sins. He assures us that he will lead us to the heights of heaven. What more could we possibly want? So many times the allurements of the world cloud our vision and we forget about God's promises. Be sure to remind the children to ask forgiveness of their sins. Pray an Act of Contrition with them today during your family prayers, and if you haven't already, schedule a time for confession soon. The sacrament brings great peace and strength for the journey ahead.

Family Prayer

All make the Sign of the Cross.

> *Parent*: Dear Jesus, help us keep our eyes on you. Please forgive us of our sins. Now let us listen to these words of St. John Paul II.

A parent or child reads the opening quotation aloud.

> *All*: Blessed Mother Mary, bring us closer to your Son, Jesus.

> St. John Paul II, please pray for us. Amen.

A Story from St. John Paul II's Life

Pope John Paul II wanted to see the people of Mexico firsthand. He had set out to bring Christian attention to the poor in Mexico and to offer them his guidance in dealing with their social and economic conditions. He spoke to countless people—workers, farmers—expressing his sympathy and understanding.

The pontiff brought up another timely subject. He said, "We cannot shut our eyes to the plight of those who abandon their homeland in search of employment . . . and often have to live in conditions unworthy of human beings."[5]

Pope John Paul II aimed to inspire the bishops of Latin America to be mindful of bringing peace and justice to their people and to work hard to implement new ways to carry out the Church's mission.

Fasting

Today, fast from complaining. Remind the children that there is far too much to be thankful for, so we should not be discontented.

Almsgiving

Take time to think of someone who could use your help in some way and encourage the kids to do the same.

Prayer

Today's Intention: Let's pray for all those who live in conditions unworthy of human beings.

Closing Prayer: Dear Jesus, draw us closer and closer to you.

All pray the Our Father, Hail Mary, and Glory Be.

All through the Day: Jesus is my redemption, my way, my resurrection, my light, my salvation, and my king!

FRIDAY, THIRD WEEK OF LENT

Lent will help us return to ourselves and courageously renounce whatever prevents us from faithfully following the Gospel. Especially in these days let us contemplate the image of the Father embracing the son who returned to his paternal home.

—General Audience, February 17, 1999

Parent Reflection

As parents, you may at times just shake your head in amazement over your children's antics. They are a work in progress, after all, as are we. Life is an interesting spiritual journey in which God in his loving providence gives us many opportunities to help others and ourselves by turning fully to God with all of our needs. St. John Paul II encourages us to courageously renounce whatever it is that separates us from God. Let's take some time today to ponder our lives through prayer.

Family Prayer

All make the Sign of the Cross.

Parent: Dear Jesus, help us give you anything that separates us from you. Weed it out of us. Now let us listen to these words of St. John Paul II.

A parent or child reads the opening quotation aloud.

All: Blessed Mother Mary, bring us closer to your Son, Jesus.

St. John Paul II, please pray for us. Amen.

A Story from St. John Paul II's Life

On March 4, 1979, Pope John Paul II's first encyclical letter, *Redemptor Hominis* (The Redeemer of Man), was published. He wrote about his intentions on shepherding the Church, and he discussed some focal points of his papal ministry, his position on Church policies, and his views on world affairs. His first formal writing as pope focused on the welfare of the people of the world. He emphasized and deplored inequality based on economic and social injustices and highlighted the importance of respect for human rights and the sanctity of human life. He also pointed out the need to preserve the earth's resources and to control technology.

Pope John Paul II spelled out his willingness to share his rule of the Church jointly with his bishops. He underscored his desire to take the truth of the Gospel to all mankind by preaching throughout the world as Jesus had instructed his disciples. Many saw his statement as a declaration that would make the Church something truly for all people.

Fasting

Today, ask the whole family to fast from a special treat or a favorite game or activity.

Almsgiving

With the children, give some time in prayer for the poor today.

Prayer

> *Today's Intention*: Let's pray for the poor and unfortunate.

> *Closing Prayer*: Dear Jesus, help us help others.

> *All pray the Our Father, Hail Mary, and Glory Be.*

> *All through the Day*: I need to follow the Gospel wholeheartedly.

FOURTH SUNDAY OF LENT

The parable of the prodigal son, in which Jesus wanted to tell us of the heavenly Father's tender mercy, becomes powerfully eloquent. There are three key stages in the story of this young man with whom, in a certain sense, each of us can identify when we yield to temptation and fall into sin.

The first stage: the distancing. We distance ourselves from God, like that son from his father, when we forget that the goods and talents we possess were given to us by God as a task and we thoughtlessly squander them. Sin is always a waste of our humanity, a waste of very precious values such as the dignity of the person and the inheritance of divine grace.

The second stage is the *process of conversion*. Man, who by sin voluntarily left his Father's house, realizes what he lost and gradually makes the decisive step of coming to himself: "I will arise and go to my Father" (Lk 15:18). The certainty that God "is good and loves me" is stronger than shame and discouragement: it sheds new light on one's sense of guilt and personal unworthiness.

Lastly, *the third stage: the return*. The one important thing for the father is that his son has been found. The embrace between him and the prodigal son becomes a celebration of forgiveness and joy. This is a moving Gospel scene that reveals in full detail the attitude of our Father in heaven, who is "rich in mercy" (cf. Eph 2:4).

—*General Audience, February 17, 1999*

Parent Reflection

Today is the Fourth Sunday of Lent. All of the gospel readings for the Church's three cycles of Lent offer perspectives on Jesus, the Light of the World. Cycle A is about the man born blind, Jesus meets Nicodemus at night in Cycle B, and the story of the prodigal son is in Cycle C.

Do we distance ourselves from God? Think about that today. Can you endeavor to seek Jesus out today—to look for his light? We don't want to hide our sins in darkness but to reveal our failings in the light in full surrender to God. Encourage the family to use Lent wisely and to strive to seek out Jesus in a deeper way.

Family Prayer

All *make the Sign of the Cross.*

Parent: Dear Jesus, forgive us of our sins and failings. Now let us listen to these words of St. John Paul II.

A *parent or child reads the opening quotation aloud.*

All: Blessed Mother Mary, bring us closer to your Son, Jesus.

St. John Paul II, please pray for us. Amen.

A Story from St. John Paul II's Life

A few months after releasing his first encyclical letter, Pope John Paul II set out in June on another pilgrimage. This one was to his dear homeland, Poland, a blessed nine-day visit. The Polish people were very enthused and proud that the new pope was from their own land. But some looked forward to his trip with trepidation because of the prevalent unrest; to arrange this trip, negotiations between Church authorities and the representatives of the People's Republic of Poland and its Communist party needed to be put into place. The Church was told that the trip must be only of a spiritual nature with no political agenda.

Millions of admirers enthusiastically greeted Pope John Paul II, and many openly wept. The excited people threw flowers, carried banners, and sang loudly both religious and national songs despite the opposing police orders. Pope John Paul II planted seeds for the foundation of the labor movement Solidarity.

A few years later, in 1983, he had words with Poland's leader, General Wojciech Jaruzelski, who viewed the pope's visit as a threat to Soviet communism. He knew that the pope carried a powerful message of human dignity, with which the general and the Communist party were at great odds.

Fasting

Today, fast from wanting things to go your way. Pray, "Jesus, your way, not mine." Ask the children to try this as well.

Almsgiving

Give fifteen minutes to someone today. Call up a needy friend or relative or help someone with a chore at home. Encourage the kids to help a sibling or friend, too.

Prayer

Today's Intention: Let's pray for the lonely and forgotten.

Closing Prayer: Dear Jesus, help us spread your love everywhere.

All pray the Our Father, Hail Mary, and Glory Be.

All through the Day: Jesus wants to welcome me from my sin with open arms.

MONDAY, FOURTH WEEK OF LENT

How many people throughout the ages have recognized in this parable [of the prodigal son] the basic elements of their own story? The way that leads back to the Father's house after the bitter experience of sin comes through an examination of conscience, repentance, and the firm intention to be converted. It is an interior process that changes the way one looks at reality; it makes a person realize his own frailty and it spurs the believer to throw himself into God's arms. When man, supported by grace, goes over these steps in his mind, he feels an acute need to rediscover himself and his own dignity as a son in the Father's embrace.

—*General Audience, February 17, 1999*

Parent Reflection

Sometimes it's tough to remember and recognize God outside the doors of our domestic church (unless we are at church). Our culture makes it difficult. We can easily get distracted. But the road to heaven is narrow and our time here on earth is shorter than we may realize. We must make the most of it and raise our little saints to heaven! Parents have a very important mission and each day counts a lot. Use this day to bring God into your home with your teachings and love.

Family Prayer

All make the Sign of the Cross.

> *Parent:* Dear Jesus, help our family grow in holiness and please you. Now let us listen to these words of St. John Paul II.

A parent or child reads the opening quotation aloud.

> *All:* Blessed Mother Mary, bring us closer to your Son, Jesus.

> St. John Paul II, please pray for us. Amen.

A Story from St. John Paul II's Life

While in Poland, Pope John Paul II's presence challenged the Communist authorities. He expected from them the full religious freedom noted in the state's constitution. He celebrated several Masses in public squares and spoke to an abundance of young people. The pope appealed to the youth that without Christ in their lives they could not see beyond the materialism of the twentieth century. The Holy Father would continue to address the youth throughout his pontificate.

On June 4, 1979, a helicopter brought him from Gniezno to Czestochowa. More than five hundred thousand were waiting to see him. He went to the Monastery of Jasna Gora ("bright mountain") where the famous shrine of the ancient wooden icon of Our Lady of Czestochowa is kept. That day at noon, the beloved pope celebrated a Mass that would last for three hours. At the elevation of the host, Pope John Paul II reverently consecrated himself and the whole Church to Mother Mary. The massive congregation fell to their knees at that pivotal moment.

Fasting

Today, ask the family to fast from technology as much as possible.

Almsgiving

Encourage the children to draw a picture (the young ones) or write a poem (the older ones) to be given to a shut-in or elderly relative or neighbor.

Prayer

Today's Intention: Let's pray for the elderly, that they may turn fully to God.

Closing Prayer: Dear Jesus, thank you for our family. Our Lady of Czestochowa, pray for us and the whole world.

All pray the Our Father, Hail Mary, and Glory Be.

All through the Day: God would like me to throw myself into his arms.

TUESDAY, FOURTH WEEK OF LENT

"Father, I have sinned . . . before you" (Lk 15:18). In the season of Lent, these words inspire strong feelings, since this is
a time when the ecclesial community is invited to profound
conversion. If it is true that sin closes man to God, on the
other hand, a sincere confession of sins reawakens his conscience to the regenerating action of God's grace. In effect,
man is not restored to friendship with God until the words
"Father, I have sinned" flow from his lips and his heart.
—*General Audience, February 17, 1999*

Parent Reflection

The life of a parent is truly an interesting journey. We never truly
know how our children's lives will unfold. But we do know that
by offering them a firm fundamental foundation of faith, hope, and
love, they will be strengthened in their resolve to lead Christian lives.
We know that the world outside the doors of our domestic church
is not always so friendly. We must make the time when our children
are young to nurture their faith and teach them how to navigate their
lives and to resist temptation.

Family Prayer

All make the Sign of the Cross.

Parent: Dear Jesus, we love you. Strengthen our family
in your love. Now let us listen to these words of St.
John Paul II.

A parent or child reads the opening quotation aloud.

All: Blessed Mother Mary, bring us closer to your Son,
Jesus.

St. John Paul II, please pray for us. Amen.

A Story from St. John Paul II's Life

Pope John Paul II was asked to visit Ireland but there was the ongoing strife between Northern Ireland and the south to worry about. When plans were being made for Pope John Paul II to go to the United States, Irish bishops and civil leaders wanted to seize the opportunity to see if they could persuade the pope to squeeze in a visit. Negotiations were necessary, but then it was settled—he would go to Ireland, even visiting Northern Ireland in the archdiocese of Armagh.

Not everyone was happy about the idea. Presbyterian minister Ian Paisley said in no uncertain terms that the pope would not be welcomed in Northern Ireland. Suddenly, a highly esteemed war hero, Lord Louis, was assassinated and then eighteen British soldiers were killed by the IRA (Irish Republican Army). The British asked the pope to stay away from Northern Ireland. After advice and wise counsel, he decided not to visit the north. Rather, he flew into Dublin airport. He said he hoped to "change the atmosphere of tension" which "provoked lacerations and also, sad to say, ruin and death."

Fasting

Today, fast from worrying and ask the kids to try to do this, too.

Almsgiving

Offer all of your worries and concerns to God today and encourage the children to do the same.

Prayer

> *Today's Intention*: Let's pray for all who are enduring heartache and pain.
>
> *Closing Prayer*: Dear Jesus, help us help others.
>
> *All pray the Our Father, Hail Mary, and Glory Be.*
>
> *All through the Day*: God invites me to a profound conversion.

WEDNESDAY, FOURTH WEEK OF LENT

▌▌

Christ chose to lower himself from glory to death on a cross.
—*General Audience, August 4, 2004*

Parent Reflection

Our Lord calls parents to aspire to be instruments of love, peace, compassion, and forgiveness. Christian parents care about their children's eternal salvation, not merely the needs of the here and now. So, at times, your love as a Christian parent may seem radical to a non-Christian, who does not share your views. And sometimes, your children might feel that your love is intense because you care so much for their eternal salvation. God will continue to inspire you to raise your children with an abiding love. Ask for God's graces to do your job well.

Family Prayer

All make the Sign of the Cross.

Parent: Dear Jesus, help us appreciate your great love for us—loving us through death on a cross. Now let us listen to these words of St. John Paul II.

A parent or child reads the opening quotation aloud.

All: Blessed Mother Mary, bring us closer to your Son, Jesus.

St. John Paul II, please pray for us. Amen.

A Story from St. John Paul II's Life

Pope John Paul II made his first visit to North America in 1979. He arrived at Logan International Airport and was greeted by the archbishop of Boston, who climbed right up the stairs to see the Holy Father. After a short embrace, the pontiff descended the stairs, knelt down, and kissed the ground. This ancient symbolism became an expected gesture from the Holy Father. Dignitaries, the first lady, Rosalynn Carter, and others were nearby to greet Pope John Paul II.

After greeting the huge crowds along his motorcade throughout the city, the pope celebrated holy Mass on the Boston Common. More than ten thousand youth surrounded the altar. About forty thousand people were assembled for Mass, which the Holy Father celebrated in honor of St. Thérèse of the Child Jesus since it was October 1, her feast day. During his homily, Pope John Paul II said, "I greet you, America the Beautiful." The crowd cheered, *"Viva il Papa!"* The beloved pope asked the youth to follow Christ and not escapism. "This is why I have come to Boston tonight: to call you to Christ—to call all of you and each of you to live in His body, today and forever. Amen!"[6]

Fasting

Today, fast from selfishness or thinking about oneself. Ask the children to instead reach out to others.

Almsgiving

Give away time today. Ponder ways you and the kids can brighten someone's day.

Prayer

Today's Intention: Let's pray for all prisoners and prisoners of war.

Closing Prayer: Dear Jesus, help us radiate your love to others.

All pray the Our Father, Hail Mary, and Glory Be.

All through the Day: Jesus wants me to shine his light in all I do.

THURSDAY, FOURTH WEEK OF LENT

On this last stretch of our penitential journey, may we be accompanied by Mary, the Virgin who remained ever faithful beside the Son, especially during the days of the Passion. May she teach us to love "to the end" following in the footsteps of Jesus, who saved the world through his Death and his Resurrection.

—*General Audience, April 11, 2001*

Parent Reflection

Just in the course of one day, we complain many times about our situations and circumstances or even little annoyances. Today, take some time with your family to ponder all of the sufferings our Lord endured during his passion and crucifixion. Take a few moments to gaze upon a crucifix. Meditating on Jesus' great love for us should cause us to reconsider all of our complaining. Ask the children to express what they are thankful to Jesus for.

Family Prayer

All make the Sign of the Cross.

> *Parent*: Dear Jesus, thank you for dying for us. Now let us listen to these words of St. John Paul II.

A parent or child reads the opening quotation aloud.

> *All*: Blessed Mother Mary, bring us closer to your Son, Jesus.

> St. John Paul II, please pray for us. Amen.

A Story from St. John Paul II's Life

In New York City, Pope John Paul II would arrive to about two thousand people on the tarmac at the airport, where he was welcomed by the UN secretary-general, Kurt Waldheim. Later, an estimated five million admirers greeted him along the parade routes. He arrived at the United Nations to a high-spirited crowd. After greeting and hugging and kissing many children nearby, he conferred with dignitaries and then delivered his address.

This peaceful pope stated that the United Nations was in existence to unify, not to divide. He often alluded to the "universal" value of human life. He again mentioned his appeal for an end to war. He said it was necessary to make a continual effort to stop provoking war. "All human beings," he expressed, "in every nation and country should be able to enjoy effectively their full rights under any political regime or system."[7] Pope John Paul II received a standing ovation from the delegates.

Fasting

Today, fast from complaining and negativity and ask the children to do so also.

Almsgiving

Take some time to thank Jesus for his great love for your family. Find a way to thank him concretely as a family by helping others, showing God's love.

Prayer

Today's Intention: Let's pray for the persecuted and tortured people all over the world.

Closing Prayer: Dear Jesus, forgive us of our sins. Help us live holy lives.

All pray the Our Father, Hail Mary, and Glory Be.

All through the Day: Jesus loves me so much that he died for me.

FRIDAY, FOURTH WEEK OF LENT

From the paradox of the Cross springs the answer to our most worrying questions. *Christ suffers for us.* He takes upon himself the sufferings of everyone and redeems them. *Christ suffers with us,* enabling us to share our pain with him. United to the suffering of Christ, human suffering becomes a means of salvation.

—*Message for the World Day of Sick, February 11, 2004*

Parent Reflection

To live out a Christian life is really a fascinating adventure. The Church teaches us that we can offer our sufferings to Jesus, uniting them to him, and they will become a means to salvation. Pope John Paul II explained this on the World Day of Sick in 2004: "Pain, accepted with faith, becomes the doorway to the mystery of the Lord's redemptive suffering; a suffering that no longer takes away peace and happiness since it is illuminated by the splendor of the Resurrection." This is truly amazing and comforting. So, let's not waste our suffering and pain. Let's lovingly offer it to Jesus and teach our children to do so as well.

Family Prayer

All make the Sign of the Cross.

Parent: Dear Jesus, help us to lovingly offer our sufferings and pain to you. Please grant our family all of the graces we need to lead a holy life. Now let us listen to these words of St. John Paul II.

A parent or child reads the opening quotation aloud.

All: Blessed Mother Mary, bring us closer to your Son, Jesus.

St. John Paul II, please pray for us. Amen.

A Story from St. John Paul II's Life

The Holy Father visited Harlem and the South Bronx while he was in New York. Later on, he celebrated Mass with an estimated eighty thousand people in Yankee Stadium, warning them during his homily of the dangers of excessive materialism. He told the crowd to break away from the temptation of involvement in mass consumerism, which he said is "exhausting and joyless." He explained that to do so "is not a question of slowing down progress, for there is no human progress when everything conspires to give full rein to self-interest, sex, and power."[8]

Pope John Paul II spoke about the parable of the rich man and Lazarus, reminding them that God didn't condemn the rich man because of his wealth but because he was selfish. "God curses selfishness," he said. He was surely not a man to mince words.

Fasting

Today, fast from selfishness and ask the children to do this, too.

Almsgiving

Give generously of your time today. It's hard to give up time when you are busy, but prayerfully give your time away to help others. Ask the children to do something kind for another.

Prayer

Today's Intention: Let's pray for families everywhere.

Closing Prayer: Dear Jesus, help us help others.

All pray the Our Father, Hail Mary, and Glory Be.

All through the Day: I shouldn't waste my sufferings.

FIFTH SUNDAY OF LENT

However tiring, the road to Emmaus leads from a sense of discouragement and bewilderment to the fullness of Easter faith. In retracing this journey, we, too, are joined by the mysterious traveling Companion. Jesus approaches us on the road, meeting us where we are and asking us the essential questions that open the heart to hope. He has many things to explain about his and our destiny. In particular, he reveals that every human life must pass through his Cross to enter into glory. But Christ does something more: he breaks the bread of sharing for us, offering that Eucharistic Table in which the Scriptures acquire their full meaning and reveal the unique and shining features of the Redeemer's face.

—*General Audience, April 18, 2001*

Parent Reflection

Today is the Fifth Sunday of Lent. In the three gospels in the Church's cycle, we learn about the raising of Lazarus (Jn 11:1–45), Jesus speaking about his coming death (Jn 12:20–33), and the story of the woman caught in adultery (Jn 8:1–11).

Jesus says, "Amen, Amen, I say to you, unless a grain of wheat falls to the ground and dies, it remains just a grain of wheat; but if it dies, it produces fruit" (Jn 12:24). Lazarus's rising from the dead was a sign of this. Lazarus was not resurrected as Jesus was; he was resuscitated. It points to Jesus' rising and his power to raise us from our sin and bring us new life. The woman caught in adultery was forgiven of her sins and also raised to new life. Jesus is loving and merciful.

Jesus comes to meet us all throughout our lives, each and every day. As St. John Paul II says above, "Jesus approaches us on the road, meeting us where we are and asking us the essential questions that open the heart to hope." In what areas of our lives might we be lacking in hope? Sometimes we might feel a bit frustrated or down because we are feeling extra challenged. St. John Paul II reminds us that Jesus "reveals that every human life must pass through his Cross to enter into glory." Strive to accept the sufferings and challenges that are sprinkled throughout your days—both the big ones and the small ones—trusting that the Divine Physician knows what is best for you.

Family Prayer

All make the Sign of the Cross.

> *Parent*: Dear Jesus, help us recognize you in our lives. Now let us listen to these words of St. John Paul II.

A parent or child reads the opening quotation aloud.

> *All*: Blessed Mother Mary, bring us closer to your Son, Jesus.

> St. John Paul II, please pray for us. Amen.

A Story from St. John Paul II's Life

The excited crowds continued to greet the holy pontiff with cheers, flowers, and long streamers of ticker tape. Even downpours of rain didn't dampen the spirits of thousands upon thousands who came out to see and hear from Pope John Paul II. It was off to Brooklyn and Saint James Cathedral, and then he would bid farewell to the New York City crowds and make his way to Philadelphia, the place where the United States was born through the Declaration of Independence.

As the Holy Father descended the steps of his plane, "Shepherd One," crowds of parochial grade-school students greeted the pope holding signs and bearing yellow chrysanthemums. Next, he went to the Cathedral of Saints Peter and Paul while exuberant crowds—at least a million of them—waved and shouted, apparently not able to contain their joy upon seeing their shepherd.

Fasting

Today, fast from rushing around. If possible, schedule a time for the family to rest in God's love by seeking a bit of silence to pray and ponder about his great love for you.

Almsgiving

Give God your time today. Pray for others and ask the children to do so as well.

Prayer

Today's Intention: Let's pray for the poorest of the poor all over the world.

Closing Prayer: Dear Jesus, help us grow in holiness.

All pray the Our Father, Hail Mary, and Glory Be.

All through the Day: Jesus loves me!

MONDAY, FIFTH WEEK OF LENT

It was the last evening of his earthly life and in the Upper Room, Jesus was about to offer the best morsel to Judas, the traitor. He thought back to this phrase in the Psalm ["Even my friend, in whom I trusted, who ate my bread, has turned against me" (Ps 41:10)], which is indeed the supplication of a sick man, abandoned by his friends. In this ancient prayer, Christ found the words and sentiments to express his own deep sorrow.

—*General Audience, June 2, 2004*

Parent Reflection

Do we endeavor to offer the "best morsel" to our enemy? I don't think so. Jesus did so with Judas in the upper room. In reality, we are more apt to save the best morsel for ourselves. Take some time and ponder how you can think less of yourself and more of someone else. Talk to the kids about sharing and caring for one another's salvation. Reward their generous behavior with warm hugs.

Family Prayer

All make the Sign of the Cross.

> *Parent*: Dear Jesus, help us focus more on others than on ourselves. Now let us listen to these words of St. John Paul II.

A parent or child reads the opening quotation aloud.

> *All*: Blessed Mother Mary, bring us closer to your Son, Jesus.

> St. John Paul II, please pray for us. Amen.

A Story from St. John Paul II's Life

The trips were exhausting, but the Holy Father enjoyed them immensely. His message consistently penetrated the crowds. While in Philadelphia, he spoke about freedom and human values. He emphasized that freedom cannot be seen as "a pretext for moral anarchy." He condemned the modern-day inclination toward "laxity regarding the Christian view on sexuality." He said, "Moral values do not militate against the freedom of the person . . . on the contrary, they exist precisely for that freedom, since they are given to insure the right use of freedom."

Fasting

Today, fast from your favorite pastime or treat and ask the children to try to do this, too.

Almsgiving

Give the "best morsel" to someone else today. Help the children to decide how they will accomplish this.

Prayer

> *Today's Intention*: Let's pray for the holy souls in purgatory.
>
> *Closing Prayer*: Dear Jesus, help us share our "best morsels" with others.
>
> *All pray the Our Father, Hail Mary, and Glory Be.*
>
> *All through the Day*: It's not about me.

TUESDAY, FIFTH WEEK OF LENT

Let us be captivated, then, by the fascination of Christ's Resurrection. May the Virgin Mary help us to experience in full the joy of Easter: a joy which, as the Risen One promised, no one can ever take from us and which will never end (cf. Jn 16:22).

—*General Audience, April 18, 2001*

Parent Reflection

E aster is fast approaching, but we still must get through some final days in our penitential journey. We can hang on to the great hope of the Resurrection. St. John Paul II reminds us that the joy we will receive because of the Resurrection is a profound Easter joy that no one can take from us. Try to keep this in mind when you undergo daily challenges in raising a family in our day and age. Remind yourself that the joy that God gives to Christians is never ending and no one can take it from you. Allow joy to live in your heart today and always. Teach the children to strive to have a joyful heart.

Family Prayer

All make the Sign of the Cross.

Parent: Dear Jesus, thank you for all of your blessings and love. Now let us listen to these words of St. John Paul II.

A parent or child reads the opening quotation aloud.

All: Blessed Mother Mary, bring us closer to your Son, Jesus.

St. John Paul II, please pray for us. Amen.

A Story from St. John Paul II's Life

Pope John Paul II engaged in more meetings with the People of God and leaders of nations than any of his predecessors. He had more than 1,160 General Audiences, which were held on Wednesdays, in addition to other audiences and religious ceremonies. Millions of the faithful met him during his pastoral visits throughout the world. This hands-on pontiff made thirty-eight official visits with government personalities and held 738 audiences and meetings with heads of states and 246 audiences with prime ministers.

Fasting

Today, fast from reacting negatively to things that fill your day. Ask the kids to try their best to be positive, too.

Almsgiving

Encourage the kids to draw a smiley face for each time they smile sincerely at someone today.

Prayer

Today's Intention: Let's pray for peace in the world.

Closing Prayer: Dear Jesus, help us spread your joy.

All pray the Our Father, Hail Mary, and Glory Be.

All through the Day: God wants me to spread his joy. Peace can begin with a smile.

WEDNESDAY, FIFTH WEEK OF LENT

After recognizing and contemplating the face of the risen Christ, we too, like the two disciples, are asked to run to our brothers and sisters to bring everyone the great news: "We have seen the Lord!" (Jn 20:25).

—*General Audience, April 18, 2001*

Parent Reflection

We can strive to see the Lord in our children each and every day—and in our spouses, too. We are instructed in the Gospel of Matthew 25:31–46 that we are to serve Jesus in one another, and that whatever we do or do not do to others, we do to Jesus. And further, when we die we will be judged by how much we have loved. "Truly I tell you, just as you did it to one of the least of these who are members of my family, you did it to me." Take some time today and ponder what this means to you. Talk to the kids about it.

Family Prayer

All make the Sign of the Cross.

Parent: Dear Jesus, help us see you in our family members and everyone. Now let us listen to these words of St. John Paul II.

A parent or child reads the opening quotation aloud.

All: Blessed Mother Mary, bring us closer to your Son, Jesus.

St. John Paul II, please pray for us. Amen.

A Story from St. John Paul II's Life

Pope John Paul II had such a love for young people. You could see it on his expressive face whenever he engaged with them. He knew in his heart that the youth were the future of the Church and that they were up against so much evil from the culture. He wanted to protect them and guide them closer to Jesus. The beloved pontiff established

World Youth Day to gather millions of the world's youth in holy pilgrimages to help transform hearts and souls. He celebrated nineteen World Youth Days during his pontificate. Pope John Paul II also knew that he had to evangelize the family, which was so much in need of guidance and encouragement. So in 1994, he established the World Meetings of Families.

Fasting

Today, fast from bickering. When tempted to argue, offer a prayer for the person instead. Help the kids with this.

Almsgiving

Give at least ten minutes of your time in quiet prayer and encourage the children to try to do so as well.

Prayer

Today's Intention: Let's pray for priests and religious.

Closing Prayer: Dear Jesus, help our family serve you more lovingly each day.

All pray the Our Father, Hail Mary, and Glory Be.

All through the Day: Life is precious. God wants me to serve others.

The laity can accomplish their proper vocation in the world and attain holiness not only through their active involvement in helping the poor and needy, but also by imbuing society with a Christian spirit as they carry out their professional duties and offer an example of Christian family life. Here I am thinking not only of leaders in public life but also of the many people who can transform their daily life into prayer, placing Christ at the center of their activity. He will draw them all to Himself and satisfy their hunger and thirst for righteousness (Mt 5:6).

—*Address, December 3, 2005*

Parent Reflection

As parents, we should be placing Christ at the center of our homes and lives. That's not always easy as we grapple with the various challenges of our society. It sometimes seems as if so much is going on around us and causing us to lose sight of the big picture. But let us endeavor to keep Christ at the center, and everything can fall into place after that. Christ is first. Talk to the kids about turning to God first with everything.

Family Prayer

All make the Sign of the Cross.

> *Parent:* Dear Jesus, guide us ever closer to you each day. Please grant us the graces we need. Now let us listen to these words of St. John Paul II.

A parent or child reads the opening quotation aloud.

> *All:* Blessed Mother Mary, bring us closer to your Son, Jesus.

> St. John Paul II, please pray for us. Amen.

A Story from St. John Paul II's Life

Pope John Paul II promised a spiritual renewal in the Church by encouraging prayer meetings of peace, dialogue with the Jews and other religions, and Apostolic Letters and instructions regarding the future path of the Church. He established the Year of Redemption, the Marian Year, and the Year of the Eucharist, and he guided the Church into the third millennium.

A prolific writer, often writing laboriously in longhand, and not one to rest from matters of the Faith, this holy pontiff wrote many important documents, including fourteen encyclicals, fifteen Apostolic Exhortations, eleven Apostolic Constitutions, and forty-five Apostolic Letters.

Fasting

Today, fast from judging others. Talk to the kids about not judging people on their clothing or the color of their skin.

Almsgiving

Encourage the children to tangibly show God's love to someone today who might not be expecting a surprise phone call, a note, a card, or some little act of service.

Prayer

Today's Intention: Let's pray for all unbelievers, especially for those who show hatred toward the Church.

Closing Prayer: Dear Jesus, help us love with your love.

All pray the Our Father, Hail Mary, and Glory Be.

All through the Day: God loves me with an everlasting love!

It is above all in raising children that the family fulfills its mission to proclaim the gospel of life. By word and example, in the daily round of relations and choices, and through concrete actions and signs, parents lead their children to authentic freedom, actualized in the sincere gift of self, and they cultivate in them respect for others, a sense of justice, cordial openness, dialogue, generous service, solidarity, and all other values that help people to live life as a gift.

—*Evangelium Vitae (The Gospel of Life)*, 92.4

Parent Reflection

Word and example are powerful. Children are like little sponges. Our example speaks volumes to them. Our domestic church should be a place where the virtues are practiced heroically within the give and take and nitty-gritty details of family life. Take some time today to ponder how your words, example, and actions are (or aren't) guiding your children toward heaven. Talk to the children about their words and actions, too. Help them understand the importance of thinking before speaking or acting and why they should do everything to please God.

Family Prayer

All make the Sign of the Cross.

Parent: Dear Jesus, please guide us to remember that all we do and say can either help or hurt others. Now let us listen to these words of St. John Paul II.

A parent or child reads the opening quotation aloud.

All: Blessed Mother Mary, bring us closer to your Son, Jesus.

St. John Paul II, please pray for us. Amen.

A Story from St. John Paul II's Life

While constantly in a spirit of prayer, Pope John Paul II accomplished a great deal. He published five books of his own: *Crossing the Threshold of Hope* (1994), *Gift and Mystery: On the Fiftieth Anniversary of My Ordination as Priest* (1996), *Roman Triptych: Poetic Meditations* (2003), *Arise, Let Us Be Going* (2004), and *Memory and Identity* (2005). Pope John Paul II was the first pope to enter into the main synagogue in Rome and first to set foot in a mosque. He was by far the most traveled pope. He visited more than one hundred nations and kissed the ground upon reaching each one.

Fasting

Today, fast from saying or doing anything negative or hurtful. Help the kids with this.

Almsgiving

Give away ten or fifteen minutes of time by doing a chore to help someone in the family or a needy neighbor and encourage the children to assist in this, too.

Prayer

Today's Intention: Let's pray for all who have lost their faith.

Closing Prayer: Dear Jesus, help us spread your love to everyone we meet.

All pray the Our Father, Hail Mary, and Glory Be.

All through the Day: My words and actions can help or hurt.

PASSION (PALM) SUNDAY

Dear brothers and sisters, these days are particularly suitable
for intensifying the conversion of our hearts to the One who
out of love died for our sake.

—*General Audience, April 7, 2004*

Parent Reflection

Today is Palm Sunday (or Passion Sunday). It is the last Sunday in
our Lenten journey and has great significance in salvation history.
Today's feast commemorates Jesus' triumphant entry into Jerusalem
to celebrate the Passover. People rushed over to see Jesus, consider-
ing him to be their king. They laid out palm branches before him as
he rode on a donkey, fulfilling the prophesy of Zechariah: "See your
king shall come to you; a just savior is he, meek, and riding on an ass,
on a colt, the foal of an ass" (Zec 9:9). They called out, "Hosanna to
the Son of David; Blessed is he who comes in the name of the Lord!
Hosanna in the highest heaven!" (Mt 21:9).

There was much symbolism: the donkey symbolized peace, and
the palm branches signified that a dignitary or king was arriving in
glory and triumph. Through the ages, palm branches have been used
in procession on Palm Sunday and represent joy and victory. The
faithful take them and use them in their homes as sacramentals—
sometimes throwing them into a fire during storms or placing them
on graves, in fields, or in barns. Ashes from burned palms are used
for the following Ash Wednesday's ashes.

Holy Week begins today with the reading of the Passion at Mass.
We should strive to meditate on the events of the Passion throughout the coming week. This is truly the holiest of weeks, and we can
receive many graces.

Family Prayer

All make the Sign of the Cross.

Parent: Dear Jesus, please grant us the graces we need to
come closer to you and understand the Passion. Now
let us listen to these words of St. John Paul II.

A parent or child reads the opening quotation aloud.

All: Blessed Mother Mary, bring us closer to your Son, Jesus.

St. John Paul II, please pray for us. Amen.

A Story from St. John Paul II's Life

Pope John Paul II created 231 cardinals, thus greatly expanding the College of Cardinals. He called the College of Cardinals to six full meetings. A man of great vision and zeal, he organized many assemblies including fifteen assemblies of the Synod of Bishops: six Ordinary General Assemblies (in 1980, 1983, 1987, 1990, 1994, and 2001); one Extraordinary General Assembly (in 1985); and eight Special Assemblies (in 1980, 1991, 1994, 1995, 1997, two in 1998, and 1999).

Fasting

Today, fast from falling into temptations to be prideful. If you or the kids feel the urge to boast, think of ways to put the emphasis on another's good works and accomplishments.

Almsgiving

Give away a higher place. Give someone else the choice of a game, television show, story to read, or other opportunity.

Prayer

Today's Intention: Let's pray for those who don't have choices, the oppressed and prisoners.

Closing Prayer: Dear Jesus, help us light the way for others.

All pray the Our Father, Hail Mary, and Glory Be.

All through the Day: Jesus wants me to surrender my heart to him.

MONDAY OF HOLY WEEK

On Calvary, Divine Mercy manifested his face of love and forgiveness for everyone. In the Upper Room after his Resurrection, Jesus entrusted the Apostles with the task of being ministers of this mercy, a source of reconciliation among men and women.

—General Audience, April 14, 2004

Parent Reflection

Your Lenten journey is quickly coming to a close. Hopefully you and the family have grown in holiness each day, striving to be more prayerful and giving. Take time this week to pause, ponder, and pray. There are many graces to take in, people to help, and prayers to be said. Try your best to guide your children to lead a virtuous life not only throughout Lent but every day of their lives. Your teachings will form a very beautiful and firm foundation of faith for their future.

Family Prayer

All make the Sign of the Cross.

> *Parent:* Dear Jesus, help our family stay close to you and your holy Mother this Holy Week. Now let us listen to these words of St. John Paul II.

A parent or child reads the opening quotation aloud.

> *All:* Blessed Mother Mary, bring us closer to your Son, Jesus.

> St. John Paul II, please pray for us. Amen.

A Story from St. John Paul II's Life

Pope John Paul II was dedicated to a life of holiness, which was apparent in all he did and said. He also brought to light the holiness of the saints and blessed. To inspire the faithful of our time, Pope John Paul II focused on countless exemplars of holiness throughout the history of the Church, with an extraordinary impetus on canonization and beatification—far more than all previous popes together. This holy pontiff solemnly beatified 1,338 holy men and women in 147 ceremonies and canonized 482 saints during fifty-one canonization celebrations. In addition to bringing the saints and blessed to light and marking them permanently into the official Church records, Pope John Paul II solemnly declared Thérèse of the Child Jesus a Doctor of the Church (the third woman Doctor after St. Teresa of Avila and St. Catherine of Siena).

Fasting

Today, fast from being harsh and selfish. Ask the children not to be judgmental of anyone but to pray for them instead.

Almsgiving

Encourage the children to pray three Hail Marys to the Blessed Mother today. Ask them not to rush through them but to instead pray them slowly with the intention of being brought closer to Jesus through Mary.

Prayer

Today's Intention: Let's pray for families all around the world.

Closing Prayer: Dear Jesus, help our family be a wonderful Christian witness to others.

All pray the Our Father, Hail Mary, and Glory Be.

All through the Day: I pray for strength for families to stay together through prayer and love.

TUESDAY OF HOLY WEEK

‖‖

Let us allow Mary, the faithful Virgin, to accompany us; let
us reflect with her in the Upper Room and stay beside Jesus
on Calvary, to meet him risen at last on Easter Day.

—*General Audience, April 7, 2004*

Parent Reflection

Strive to include Mother Mary in all you do in the family. Ask her
to be with you and to teach you a greater holiness. Encourage the
children to call upon Mary often and for any need. St. John Paul II had
a great love for the Blessed Mother and prayed to her very often. His
words above encourage us to stay close to the faithful Virgin, reflecting with her and staying close to Jesus on Calvary. Ponder that today,
and ask Mary for the grace to better understand the great mysteries
of Jesus' suffering and death.

Family Prayer

All make the Sign of the Cross.

> *Parent*: Dear Jesus, we love you and want to grow closer
> to you this Holy Week. Now let us listen to these words
> of St. John Paul II.

A parent or child reads the opening quotation aloud.

> *All*: Blessed Mother Mary, bring us closer to your Son,
> Jesus.

St. John Paul II, please pray for us. Amen.

A Story from St. John Paul II's Life

Pope John Paul II was very devoted to the Blessed Mother. He adopted
the poignant and affectionate words *"totus tuus"* from a saint he deeply
admired and used them in his episcopal coat of arms and later in his
papal coat of arms. In his *Treatise on True Devotion to the Blessed Virgin*,
St. Louis de Montfort wrote in Latin, "I belong entirely to you (*totus*

tuus), and all that I have is yours. I take you for my all. O Mary, give me your heart." Pope John Paul II gave his pontificate to Mother Mary.

His Apostolic Letter *Rosarium Virginis Marie* (On the Most Holy Rosary) was released on October 16, 2003. The Holy Father introduced the "mysteries of light" and proclaimed a Year of the Rosary from October 2002 to October 2003, which was at the beginning of the twenty-fifth year of his pontificate.

Fasting

Today, fast from noise as much as possible. Strive to foster a peaceful atmosphere in the home. Set a timer for thirty minutes, encouraging the kids to spend quiet time in prayer and spiritual reading (which you can do together).

Almsgiving

Encourage the kids to reach out to others and to be good helpers. Is there someone who is in need in your neighborhood or community? Ponder a way you can reach out to them as a family.

Prayer

> *Today's Intention*: Let's pray for the children of the world, that they might have a loving home.
>
> *Closing Prayer*: Dear Jesus, help us spread your love.
>
> *All pray the Our Father, Hail Mary, and Glory Be.*
>
> *All through the Day*: God wants me to share generously with others.

WEDNESDAY OF HOLY WEEK

▮▮

At the heart of this sacred Triduum is the "mystery of love without limit," that is, the mystery of Jesus who "having loved his own who were in the world . . . loved them to the end" (Jn 13:1).

—*General Audience, April 11, 2001*

Parent Reflection

The sacred Triduum begins tomorrow. Talk to the children about the great holy days coming up and why they should be more aware of what these days are all about. Perhaps you can tell the story of what happened on these days, the great mystery of our salvation, at the dinner table tonight. Make preparations to attend as many of the liturgies as you can in the upcoming days.

Family Prayer

All make the Sign of the Cross.

Parent: Dear Jesus, prepare our hearts to enter into the upcoming sacred days. Please bring us closer to you. Now let us listen to these words of St. John Paul II.

A parent or child reads the opening quotation aloud.

All: Blessed Mother Mary, bring us closer to your Son, Jesus.

St. John Paul II, please pray for us. Amen.

A Story from St. John Paul II's Life

On October 19, 2003, Pope John Paul II beatified someone that he had known very personally and with whom he had discussed Church matters. It was the nun dressed in the simple cotton sari whom he had kissed atop her head after she bowed and kissed his papal ring shortly after he had become pope. The image of the tender kiss from a pope in regal vestments to a petite nun dressed in unadorned clothing was captured by photographers and appeared in newspapers the following day.

Two days after her death, Pope John Paul II said: "I have vivid memories of her diminutive figure, bent over by a life spent in the service of the poorest of the poor, but always filled with inexhaustible interior energy: the energy of Christ's love. Missionary of Charity: this is what Mother Teresa was in name and in fact" (Angelus, September 7, 1997).

Just six years after her death, at her beatification, he said: "Satiating Jesus' thirst for love and for souls in union with Mary, the Mother of Jesus, had become the sole aim of Mother Teresa's existence and the inner force that drew her out of herself and made her 'run in haste' across the globe to labor for the salvation and the sanctification of the poorest of the poor" (Homily, October 19, 2003).

Fasting

Today, fast from complaining about little sufferings or inconveniences. Say a prayer instead and ask the kids to do the same.

Almsgiving

Encourage the children to make a card, draw a picture, or write an uplifting verse to be given to someone on Easter Sunday.

Prayer

> *Today's Intention*: Let's pray for all missionaries.
>
> *Closing Prayer*: Dear Jesus, keep us close to your Sacred Heart.
>
> *All pray the Our Father, Hail Mary, and Glory Be.*
>
> *All through the Day*: My loving prayers and sacrifices can help save souls.

HOLY THURSDAY

Dear brothers and sisters, we are preparing ourselves to relive the great mystery of our salvation. Tomorrow . . . in the evening we will commemorate the *Last Supper* with the Institution of the Eucharist and of the Priesthood. The "washing of the feet" reminds us that with this gesture Jesus in the Upper Room anticipated his supreme Sacrifice on Calvary and bequeathed his love to us as a new law, *mandatum novum*. According to a pious tradition, after the rites of the Mass of the Lord's Supper, the faithful stay in adoration before the Eucharist late into the night.

—*General Audience, April 7, 2004*

Parent Reflection

Today, we commemorate the Last Supper and the institution of the Eucharist and the priesthood. Do all you can to keep this day holy. Schedule times for quiet and prayer whenever possible. Ask the Blessed Mother and your guardian angel to accompany you through the sacred Triduum so that many graces will be bestowed upon your family.

Family Prayer

All make the Sign of the Cross.

Parent: Dear Jesus, help us understand the great significance of today. Now let us listen to these words of St. John Paul II.

A parent or child reads the opening quotation aloud.

All: Blessed Mother Mary, bring us closer to your Son, Jesus.

St. John Paul II, please pray for us. Amen.

A Story from St. John Paul II's Life

On May 13, 1981 (the feast of Our Lady of Fatima), while being driven through St. Peter's Square to greet the pilgrims, Pope John Paul II was shot several times at close range by a professional assassin. Miraculously, the bullets had not touched the Holy Father's vital organs. Pope John Paul II later said that it was the Blessed Mother who had intervened to save his life. "It was a mother's hand that guided the bullet's path."

It wasn't very long after he regained consciousness that he forgave his assailant, Mehmet Ali Agca, an escaped Turkish murderer. After Pope John Paul II recuperated from his wounds, he again appeared in the same square and thanked God for allowing him "to experience suffering and the danger of losing my life." This heroic pontiff visited Agca in prison and offered him his sincere forgiveness. Before their conversation was over, Agca lowered his head and kissed Pope John Paul II's hand.

The Holy Father gave one of the bullets retrieved from his body to the bishop who oversees the shrine of Our Lady of Fatima. It was placed in the crown of the statue of the Blessed Virgin.

Fasting

Today, fast from idle or wasted time. Encourage the kids to give time to one another by helping with a chore or task.

Almsgiving

Strive to give everything to Jesus and ask the children to try to do so as well.

Prayer

Today's Intention: Let's pray for all priests.

Closing Prayer: Dear Jesus, please open our hearts and minds to hear you.

All pray the Our Father, Hail Mary, and Glory Be.

All through the Day: Mother Mary will bring me closer to Jesus.

GOOD FRIDAY

On Good Friday, the Church commemorates the passion and death of Our Lord. The Christian assembly is invited to meditate upon the evil and sin that oppress humanity and upon the salvation brought about by the redemptive Sacrifice of Christ. The Word of God and certain evocative liturgical rites, such as the Adoration of the Cross, help us to contemplate the various stages of the Passion. In addition, Christian Tradition has brought to life on this day various expressions of popular devotion. Outstanding among these are the penitential processions of Good Friday and the pious stations on the Way of the Cross, which help us to interiorize the mystery of the Cross.

—*General Audience, April 7, 2004*

Parent Reflection

What a great mystery lies within the Cross of Jesus! Today is one of the most significant days on our Church's calendar. We commemorate the day that Jesus was tortured, suffered, and died on a cross for all of us. Try your best to schedule your family's day so that you can attend church services and also observe a very quiet and prayerful day at home. Encourage the family to offer up any sufferings or sickness to God, praying that they can be united with Christ's passion. Ponder ways you might make sacrifices today without grumbling or complaining, striving to please God and help others. Consider how Mother Mary faithfully stayed with her Son until the end, offering her prayer and love. What can you learn from her?

Family Prayer

All make the Sign of the Cross.

> *Parent:* Dear Jesus, help our hearts grow to be more like yours. Now let us listen to these words of St. John Paul II.

A parent or child reads the opening quotation aloud.

All: Blessed Mother Mary, bring us closer to your Son, Jesus.

St. John Paul II, please pray for us. Amen.

A Story from St. John Paul II's Life

On April 2, 2005, at 9:37 p.m., the Church's beloved shepherd, Pope John Paul II, died. He had been a living example of a person who offers his suffering of illness to Jesus and unites it to the sufferings of the Cross to make it redemptive. It was the eve of the Octave Day of Easter and Divine Mercy Sunday, a feast that he had established.

Fasting

Follow the fasting rules for Good Friday (see the introduction to this book). Take time today to gaze upon a crucifix and pray as a family the "Prayer before a Crucifix" (see the end of this book).

Almsgiving

Is there an act of charity you can do as a family today to help a relative or neighbor?

Prayer

Today's Intention: Let's pray for the persecuted of the world and for prisoners. Ask St. Dismas, the good thief who hung alongside of Jesus, to intercede for conversions.

Closing Prayer: Dear Jesus, forgive us of our sins.

All pray the Our Father, Hail Mary, and Glory Be.

All through the Day: I can have Eternal Life because Jesus died a cruel death for me!

HOLY SATURDAY

Deep silence is a feature of Holy Saturday. In fact, no special liturgies are proposed for this day of expectation and prayer. Everything in the Church is still while the faithful, in imitation of Mary, prepare for the great event of the Resurrection.

—*General Audience, April 7, 2004*

Parent Reflection

Holy Saturday is a day of loneliness, of feeling the pangs of loss. Jesus was crucified and then sealed away in the tomb. Churches are stripped bare of everything. A quiet sadness fills the air when we have prayerfully entered into the holy Triduum. We can ponder what the disciples might have felt, missing their Messiah. They were alone and afraid. They hid in the upper room with the Blessed Mother, praying earnestly to the Holy Spirit whom Jesus had promised would come to them.

Try to find times of silence and prayer throughout the day, encouraging the family to think of Jesus and to thank him for his great love for us. Prepare your hearts in great hope for the Resurrection.

Family Prayer

All make the Sign of the Cross.

Parent: Dear Jesus, make our hearts like yours. Now let us listen to these words of St. John Paul II.

A parent or child reads the opening quotation aloud.

All: Blessed Mother Mary, bring us closer to your Son, Jesus.

St. John Paul II, please pray for us. Amen.

A Story from St. John Paul II's Life

It was a devastating moment to say the very least. The dearly loved Holy Father was dead. More than three million devoted pilgrims came to keep vigil at Pope John Paul II's side. They had first congregated below his window in the square during his final hours, praying for him and shedding tears together. Then later on, to pay homage to the remains of their beloved *Papa*, countless pilgrims waited for more than twenty-four hours to gain entrance to St. Peter's Basilica. They wanted to be near their saintly shepherd even in his death.

Fasting

Today, fast as a family from popular culture—which means no magazines, television, Internet, radio, or shopping malls.

Almsgiving

Encourage the children to offer all of their concerns and worries to God today. If they have a friend who worries a lot, pray for him or her today.

Prayer

> *Today's Intention:* Let's pray for all families, especially those who are struggling in some way.
>
> *Closing Prayer:* Dear Jesus, please allow your love to shine through us to others.
>
> *All pray the Our Father, Hail Mary, and Glory Be.*
>
> *All through the Day:* Jesus wants me to be always loving.

EASTER SUNDAY

███

The proclamation of the Resurrection scatters the darkness of the night and the whole of created reality awakens from the slumber of death to recognize Christ's lordship, as the Pauline hymn that has inspired our reflections brings to the fore: "At the name of Jesus every knee should bow, in heaven and on earth and under the earth, and every tongue confess that Jesus Christ is Lord" (Phil 2:10–11).

—*General Audience, April 7, 2004*

Parent Reflection

Happy Easter! Christ the Lord is risen today. Alleluia! We have been given a magnificent promise of new life, in this life and the next! Today is a special feast to be enjoyed with your family and celebrated with gusto. Bask in one another's company, be blessed at holy Mass, and allow the great joy of the day to permeate you through and through. Carry the holy joy into the days ahead, hanging on to Easter hope and helping to light the way for others.

Family Prayer

All make the Sign of the Cross.

> *Parent*: Dear Jesus, thank you for your great love for us! Now let us listen to these words of St. John Paul II.

A parent or child reads the opening quotation aloud.

> *All*: Blessed Mother Mary, bring us closer to your Son, Jesus.

> St. John Paul II, please pray for us. Amen.

A Story from St. John Paul II's Life

On April 28, 2005, Pope Benedict XVI announced that the normal five-year waiting period before beginning the process of the cause of beatification and canonization would be dispensed for Pope John Paul II. Some say that Pope Benedict's decision was based on the cries, "*Santo subito!*" (Sainthood now!), at Pope John Paul II's funeral Mass and on a petition signed by the cardinals who elected Pope Benedict XVI. On May 13, 2005, Pope Benedict XVI made the official announcement of the dispensation during a meeting with the Roman clergy that took place in the basilica of St. John Lateran. On June 28, 2005, Cardinal Camillo Ruini, vicar general of the Holy Father for the diocese of Rome, opened the diocesan phase of the cause of beatification and canonization of the Servant of God Pope John Paul II (Karol Wojtyla), Supreme Pontiff.

At Pope John Paul II's beatification ceremony on May 1, 2011, Pope Benedict XVI said, "He restored to Christianity its true face as a religion of hope." Pope John Paul II, sometimes called John Paul the Great, was canonized a saint on April 27, 2014.

Fasting and Almsgiving

Today is a day to celebrate. No fasting is necessary today. However, you may want to encourage the whole family to retain the spirit of prayer that was fostered in their hearts throughout the holy season of Lent. God will be very pleased with their continual sacrifices, prayers, and acts of charity offered to him in love.

Prayer

Today's Intention: Let's pray for the Church, all of its members, and all of the hierarchy. Let's continue to pray that others will convert and come into the Church.

Closing Prayer: Dear Jesus, thank you for the great blessings of our Church and our family. Help us help others.

All pray the Our Father, Hail Mary, and Glory Be.

All through the Day: Christ triumphs over evil and death. Let me be joyful and celebrate!

PRAYER BEFORE A CRUCIFIX

Look down upon me, good and gentle Jesus,
while before your face I humbly kneel and,
with burning soul,
pray and beseech you
to fix deep in my heart lively sentiments
of faith, hope, and charity;
true contrition for my sins;
and a firm purpose of amendment.
While I contemplate,
with great love and tender pity,
your five most precious wounds,
pondering over them within me
and calling to mind the words which David,
your prophet, said of you, my Jesus:
"They have pierced My hands and My feet,
they have numbered all My bones" (Ps 21:17–18).
Amen.

On the Fridays of Lent, the faithful receive a plenary indulgence if they recite the prayer before a crucifix. The indulgence is a partial indulgence any other time.

Pray these prayers for the Holy Father's intentions: Our Father, Hail Mary, and Glory Be.

NOTES

1. Chicago Tribune, *A Global Pilgrim: The Journeys of Pope John Paul II* (Ligouri, MO: Triumph Books, 2005), 14.

2. Ibid., 18.

3. Ibid., 18.

4. Francis Xavier Murphy, *The Pilgrim Pope: A Man for All Peoples* (Wapwallopen, PA: Shepherd Press, 1979), 17.

5. Ibid., 19.

6. Ibid., 64.

7. Ibid., 69.

8. Chicago Tribune, *A Global Pilgrim*, 44.

Donna-Marie Cooper O'Boyle is an award-winning author and journalist, speaker, pilgrimage host, retreat leader, and the EWTN television host of *Everyday Blessings for Catholic Moms* and *Catholic Mom's Cafe*, which she created. A Catholic wife and mother of five, Cooper O'Boyle was noted as one of the Top Ten Most Fascinating Catholics in 2009 by *Faith & Family Live*. She enjoyed a decade-long friendship with Blessed Mother Teresa of Calcutta and became a Lay Missionary of Charity. For many years her spiritual director was Servant of God John A. Hardon, S.J., who also served as one of Mother Teresa's spiritual directors.

Cooper O'Boyle was invited by the Holy See in 2008 to participate in an international congress for women at the Vatican to mark the twentieth anniversary of the apostolic letter *Mulieris Dignitatem* (On the Dignity and Vocation of Women). She received apostolic blessings from Saint John Paul II and Pope Benedict XVI on her books and work and a special blessing from Saint John Paul II for her work with Blessed Mother Teresa. Cooper O'Boyle is the author of several books on faith and family, including *Rooted in Love*, *The Miraculous Medal*, *Mother Teresa and Me*, and *Catholic Mom's Cafe*. She has been featured by Zenit news and *Rome Reports* and is a frequent guest on *EWTN Bookmark*, *Faith & Culture*, and *Vatican Insider*.